ELEMENTARY.
workbook

with key

Rob Metcalf

Contents

Grammar 1
a, an

Complete the conversation with *a* or *an*.

A: Are you good with facts?

B: Not bad. Why?

A: Let's play this game. I say (1) *a / an* name. You tell me what it is.

B: OK.

A: You have 30 seconds, starting now. What's *Wikipedia*?

B: That's easy! It's (2) *a / an* encyclopaedia on the internet.

A: Correct. What's Viru Viru?

B: No idea!

A: It's (3) *a / an* airport in Bolivia. What's Harvard?

B: It's (4) *a / an* university in the US.

A: Correct. What's Cyrillic?

B: I think it's (5) *a / an* alphabet.

A: Correct. What's Burj Al Arab?

B: Um … I don't know.

A: It's (6) *a / an* hotel in Dubai. Three correct answers. That isn't very good!

Grammar 2
Plural nouns

Complete the conversation with the plural form of the words in the box.

bus	computer	family	sandwich
university	Window		

A: Is this your computer?

B: Yes, it is. In fact, I have two (1) _____. This one uses (2) _____ XP. The other uses a different operating system.

A: And is this a photo of your family?

B: There are two (3) _____ in this photo. My family here and my cousin's in Italy.

A: And is this your brother?

B: Yes, it is. We go to different (4) _____, so he doesn't live at home now.

A: OK. Can we see the city now?

B: Sure. Three (5) _____ go from here to the city centre, so it's very quick.

A: What about lunch?

B: We can buy (6) _____ for lunch.

A: OK. Good idea.

Grammar 3A
be

Complete the blog with the correct word.

Hi again, everybody! We (1) *'m / 're / 's* in Havana now, the capital city of Cuba. It (2) *'m / 're / 's* 5 o'clock and I (3) *'m / 're / 's* at the hotel. Megan (4) *'m not / aren't / isn't* here at the moment. She's at the City Museum. There are fantastic old cars everywhere here. No, they (5) *'m not / aren't / isn't* Cuban. They (6) *'m / 're / 's* American cars from before the revolution in 1959.

That's all for today – more tomorrow. (7) *Are / You are / Are you* all OK in London? (8) *It's / Is it / It isn't* warm and sunny? It is here!

Grammar 3B
be

Complete the conversations with *am, are, aren't, is* or *isn't*.

A: (1) _____ Didier and Peter French?

B: No, they (2) _____. They're from Canada, so they speak French and English.

C: (3) _____ your phone number 313 456 719?

D: No, it (4) _____. That's my old number.

C: What's your new number?

E: Excuse me. (5) _____ you the owner of a black Toyota?

F: Yes, I (6) _____. Why?

E: I'm the owner of the house over there, and your car's in front of my garage.

Grammar 4A
Possession

Complete the conversation with the possessive adjectives in the box.

my	his	its	our	your	their

A: You're new students. What are (1) _____ names?

B: (2) _____ name's Benicio, and (3) _____ name's Cruz. We're from Mexico.

A: Hi, I'm Anders.

B: What's (4) _____ teacher's name?

Facts & Figures

A: She's called Sally.

B: And what about the other students?

A: (5) _____ names are Hannah, Jonas, Yussef and Mimi.

B: And do we need a book?

A: Yes. (6) _____ name is English Fast.

B: OK, thanks.

Grammar 4B
Possession

Complete the conversation with the correct possessive adjectives.

A: Hello. My name's Joseph, and these are my children. (1) _____ names are Gina and Tom.

B: Hi. I'm Sandra. Is there a fourth person? (2) _____ reservation's for four.

A: Yes, (3) _____ wife's coming soon. She's parking the car.

B: What's (4) _____ name?

A: Doris.

B: Well, here are (5) _____ keys.

A: Thanks. Which are (6) _____ rooms?

B: These two here. And that's my room if you have any questions.

Vocabulary 1
International words (1)

Circle the different word in each group. Read the categories to help you.

		Category
1	university radio airport hospital	Places
2	chocolate sandwich juice family	Food and drink
3	virus Windows kilometre internet	Computers
4	love yes OK no	Expressions
5	taxi golf bus	Transport

Vocabulary 2
International words (2)

Complete the puzzle.

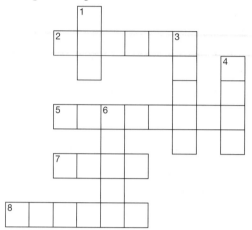

Across

2 He or she works in a hospital. (6)

5 It needs an answer! (8)

7 It's a type of photograph. You go to a hospital for this. (4)

8 Your mother, father, bothers or sisters. (6)

Down

1 You see animals in this place. (3)

3 You listen to it. (5)

4 You read it in a restaurant. (4)

6 You write and read it on a computer. (5)

Vocabulary 3
Numbers 1–10

Write the numbers as words.

1   10   _____

2   6   _____

3   4   _____

4   1   _____

5   9   _____

6   2   _____

7   5   _____

8   8   _____

9   3   _____

10   7   _____

Facts & Figures

Vocabulary 4A
Numbers 11–99

Check the sums. Are they correct (✔) or incorrect (✘)?
Circle your answer.

1	eleven + six = seventeen	✔	✘
2	fifteen + sixteen = thirty	✔	✘
3	sixty + twelve = seventy-two	✔	✘
4	thirteen + five = nineteen	✔	✘
5	forty + fifty = eighty	✔	✘
6	eighty + eighteen = ninety-eight	✔	✘

Vocabulary 4B
Numbers 11–99

Write the numbers in the sentences in words.

1 Discordians believe the number 23 is special.

_____

2 Lee's 14 years old.

_____

3 My address is 46, The High Street.

_____

4 You can drive a car when you're 18 in many countries.

_____

5 37 is my lucky number.

_____

6 Jean's number plate is JEAN 55.

_____

7 There are 12 months in the Gregorian calendar.

_____

8 89 is a number in the Fibonacci sequence.

_____

Vocabulary 5A
Ordinal numbers

Look at the table of top countries in maths. Then
complete the sentences with the ordinal numbers in the
box.

1	China	6	Taiwan
2	US	7	Hungary
3	Russia	8	Japan
4	Vietnam	9	Iran
5	Bulgaria	10	Romania

third	seventh	tenth	sixth	eighth	first	fifth
ninth	fourth	second				

1 China is _____.

2 Romania is _____.

3 Russia is _____.

4 Bulgaria is _____.

5 Japan is _____.

6 The US is _____.

Vocabulary 5B
Ordinal numbers

Write the ordinal numbers in brackets as words.

By the number of native speakers, Portuguese is possibly
the world's (1) _____ (6th) language, and
Bengali the (2) _____ (7th).

George Washington was the (3) _____ (1st)
president of the US. Barack Obama was the
(4) _____ (44th).

The Earth is the (5) _____ (3rd) planet from the
sun. Neptune is the (6) _____ (8th).

Japan is the world's (7) _____ (10th) country by
population, and Osaka is its (8) _____ (2nd) city.

E is the (9) _____ (5th) letter of the English
alphabet. I is the (10) _____ (9th) letter.

Facts & Figures

Extend your vocabulary
about

Choose the correct option, using *about* if possible.

Hi Giang,

Let me give you more information about me. I live in Ireland. It's a small country in Europe and the population is (1) *4 / about 4* million. I live in a town. It's very small, with only (2) *1/ about 1* shop – a supermarket. It's (3) *50 / about 50* kilometres from the capital city, Dublin. But my family is big. I have (4) *5 / about 5* brothers and a sister. My address is (5) *53 / about 53* The High Street, and if you phone me on Skype, the international code for Ireland is (6) *353 / about 353*.

Padraig

Vocabulary 6
Email and website addresses

1.01 Listen and choose the correct email and website addresses.

1 a peter@jsmail.com
  b peterj@smail.com
2 a sally@sallysmith.com
  b sally@sallysmith.co.uk
3 a www.kimwebb.com/index.htm
  b www.kimwebb.com/index/htm
4 a www3.factsandfigures.net
  b www.3factsandfigures.net
5 a www.newscientist.com/sectionspace
  b www.newscientist.com/section/space

Pronunciation 1
The alphabet

Match the letters 1–5 with the letters a–e that have the same sound.

1 A J   a Y
2 E P V G   b H K
3 L X Z   c S M L F
4 I   d Q
5 U W   e B T C D

1.02 Listen and check your answers.

Pronunciation 2
The alphabet

1.03 Listen to the conversations and write the names.

1 _____
2 _____
3 _____
4 _____
5 _____
6 _____
7 _____
8 _____

Listening
A talk about English

1.04 Listen to part of a talk and choose the correct options.

1 The talk is about *English history / the English alphabet / a website*.
2 The English alphabet has *26 / 40* letters.
3 The English language has *26 / 40* consonants and vowels.
4 Sh and ch *are / aren't* in the English alphabet.
5 The English alphabet and the Latin alphabet are the *same / different*.
6 The word alphabet comes from the first two letters of the *English / Greek* alphabet.

Facts & Figures

Reading
Get your facts right!

1 Can you answer these questions?

1 What's the international telephone code for South Africa?

_____

2 How high (in metres) is Mount Everest?

_____

3 How many countries are there in the world?

_____

2 Read the article. What are the answers to exercise 1?

3 Read the article again and complete the sentences.

1 Facts are easy to find today because we have

_____.

2 In the past, the main place to find information was

_____.

3 The official height of Mount Everest changed in

_____.

4 Three countries not in the United Nations are

_____.

5 To know if a fact is really true, it's important to

_____.

4 Find the words and phrases 1–5 in the article. Then match them with the definitions a–e.

1	regular	a	correct
2	right	b	obvious, not in doubt
3	clear	c	frequent, normal
4	wrong	d	see if a thing is correct
5	check	e	incorrect

5 Complete these sentences with the positive or negative form of *be*.

1 Mandarin Chinese _____ the language with the most speakers in the world.

2 B _____ the second letter of the English alphabet.

3 *Fifth* and *sixth* _____ ordinal numbers.

4 Chocolate and sandwiches _____ drinks.

5 The pronunciation of @ _____ 'at'.

Get your facts right!

Finding facts is a regular part of our work, studies and free time. What's the international phone code for South Africa? How high is Mount Everest? How many countries are there in the world? Sometimes we all need the right answer to questions like these.

Thanks to the internet, facts and figures are easier to find than in the past, when libraries were the principal place to find information. A quick search shows the answer to the first question above is 27. But online answers are not always so clear. Some websites say Everest is 8,848 metres high. Others say it's 8,850. That's because in 1999 they measured the mountain with satellite technology, and discovered that the old figure was wrong. Everest's official height is now 8,850 metres.

The third question is more difficult. Some websites say 192 – the number of countries in the United Nations (UN). But not *all* countries are in the UN. If you include the Vatican City, the answer is 193. Some websites also include Kosovo or Taiwan, but others say these countries are part of Serbia and China.

Some questions do not have easy answers. That's why it's important to compare information from different websites to check if a fact is *really* a fact.

Facts & Figures

Writing
Giving personal information

Reading

1 Read the messages from a website and answer the questions.

1 Why is English important for Silvia?

_____

_____

2 How can people communicate with Silvia?

_____

_____

3 What personal information in the welcome message isn't included in Silvia's message?

_____

_____

4 What extra information is included in her message?

_____

_____

○○○

Welcome to the English Language Meeting Point.

To join the site, complete the form below and post a message. Include information about you (your first name, surname, date of birth, address, postcode, telephone number and email address) and your interests.

○○○

Hi! My name's Silvia and I'm from Mexico. My first language is Spanish, but I need English at work. I work in a hotel. We can talk in English on the internet with a webcam. Or, if you prefer, we can communicate by Messenger, email or letter.

My main interest is music. I love Latin music, especially Latin pop and Cumbia. I'm also interested in sports. My favourite sports are tennis and football. I'm a big fan of Real Madrid. I think they're fantastic!

If you contact me, my full name's Silvia Almada and my address is Calle Coahuila 30, TIJUANA. My home email's salmada203@dmail.mx and my email address at work is almadas@mexhotels.com. I'm single and my date of birth is 24.08.1978.

Language focus: talking about interests

2 Match the sentence beginnings 1–6 to the endings a–f. Use Sylvia's message to help you.

1 My main interests _____
2 I love _____
3 I'm a fan _____
4 I think _____
5 I'm also interested _____
6 My favourite magazine _____

a modern art.
b in science.
c are art and literature.
d of Isabel Allende.
e is New Scientist.
f her books are fantastic.

Writing skills: organising information

3 Read these questions. In which paragraphs of Silvia's message are the answers? Circle your answers.

1 What are your contact details?   *1 / 2 / 3*
2 What are your interests?   *1 / 2 / 3*
3 What's your first language?   *1 / 2 / 3*
4 What's your full name and date of birth?   *1 / 2 / 3*
5 Why is English important to you?   *1 / 2 / 3*
6 How can people communicate with you?   *1 / 2 / 3*
7 What's your first name?   *1 / 2 / 3*

Preparing to write

4 Make notes on your own answers to the questions in exercise 3.

Writing

5 Write a message to post at the English Language Meeting Point website. Use your notes to help you. Organise your message into three paragraphs.

Useful phrases

- I need English at work / at university.
- I work in a hotel / at a university / for a multinational company.
- We can talk on the internet / phone.
- Or, if you prefer, we can communicate by Messenger / email / letter.
- If you contact me, …

Where & When

Grammar 1A
Prepositions (*from, in, near*)

Complete the description with the prepositions *from, in* and *near*.

Hi everyone!

My name's Mike and I'm a new member of the study group. I'm (1) _____ Newcastle (2) _____ Australia. It's a town (3) _____ Sydney. Do you know Australia? Newcastle's about 350 kilometres (4) _____ the capital city, Canberra, and it's (5) _____ a region in the south-east of the country called New South Wales.

I'm looking forward to studying with you!

Mike

Grammar 1B
Prepositions (*from, in, near*)

Complete the clues with *from, near* or *in*. Then write the name of the city.

Mystery city

1 It's _____ a European country.
2 It's about 400 kilometres _____ the capital city.
3 It's _____ a region called Alsace.
4 It's _____ a city called Stuttgart.
5 It's near Germany, but it isn't _____ Germany.
6 The Council of Europe is _____ this city.

The name of the city is _____.

Grammar 2A
Wh- questions

Put the words in the correct order to make questions.

A: (1) is / what / home town / your / ?

_____

B: It's Agra, in India.
A: That's famous. (2) famous / why / it / is / ?

_____

B: Because the Taj Mahal is there.
A: Of course! (3) the Taj Mahal / is / old / how / ?

_____

B: It's about 350 years old.

A: Wow! (4) Agra / is / where / ?

_____

B: It's in the north of India.
A: (5) like / what / it / is / ?

_____

B: It's a big, noisy city.
A: (6) a good time to visit / is / when / ?

_____

B: In October, after the Monsoon.

Grammar 2B
Wh- questions

Complete the conversations with *what, where, how old, why* or *when*.

1 A: _____ are you from?
   B: I'm from Senegal.
2 A: _____ are you?
   B: I'm twenty-eight.
3 A: _____'s Senegal like?
   B: It's a really nice country, with great people.
4 A: _____'s your email address?
   B: It's sarrtom647@yahoo.com
5 A: _____ are you in London?
   B: I'm a medical student.
6 A: _____ is our next class?
   B: On the 10th. After the Easter holidays.

Grammar 3A
Present simple (3rd person)

Complete the second sentence with the correct form of the verb in the first sentence.

Hemi and I have very different daily routines:

1 I get up at 6.30. She _____ up at 9.00.
2 I go to the gym after work. She _____ to the gym before work.
3 I start work at 8.30. She _____ work at 2.00.
4 I have lunch at work. She _____ lunch at home.
5 I finish work at 5.00. She _____ work at 8.00.
6 I watch TV after work. She _____ DVDs.

Where & When

Grammar 3B
Present simple (3rd person)

Complete the conversation with the correct form of the verbs in brackets.

A: Shall we go to the new Thai restaurant on Wednesday?

B: Wednesday isn't a good day. James (1) _____ (*finish*) work at 9.00. And I (2) _____ (*get up*) really early on Thursday.

A: What about Thursday?

B: That's not a good day either. We always (3) _____ (*go*) to the gym after work, and you normally (4) _____ (*have*) a parents' meeting at the school.

A: That's true.

B: Is Friday possible?

A: No, Olga always (5) _____ (*go*) to the cinema with her friends. What about the weekend? The restaurant (6) _____ (*open*) at lunchtime. We could have lunch there.

B: Good idea!

Grammar 4A
Present simple (negative)

Complete the sentences with the negative form of the verb in brackets.

1 September _____ (*have*) 31 days.
2 I _____ (*celebrate*) the New Year on January 1.
3 The language school _____ (*open*) on Sunday.
4 My teacher _____ (*work*) in the morning.
5 We _____ (*go*) to the gym at the weekend.
6 You _____ (*get*) up early!

Grammar 4B
Present simple (negative)

Complete the text with the negative form of the verb in brackets.

Leap years

In the Gregorian calendar, every fourth year is a leap year. Leap years (1) _____ (*have*) 365 days – they have 366. The explanation for this is that the earth (2) _____ (*take*) exactly 365 days to go round the sun – it takes about 6 hours longer. Because of this, every four years February (3) _____ (*have*) 28 days – it has 29. The 29th is called Leap Day.

The Chinese calendar (4) _____ (*follow*) the sun – it follows the sun *and* the moon. So leap years in China (5) _____ (*add*) an extra day, they add an extra month. The Hindu calendar adds an extra month too. As for the Islamic calendar, it (6) _____ (*use*) leap days or months.

Vocabulary 1
Nationalities (1)

Complete the nationalities with –*an*, –*ese*, or –*ish*.

Country	Nationality word
1 America	Americ_____
2 Brazil	Brazili_____
3 China	Chin_____
4 Germany	Germ_____
5 Japan	Japan_____
6 Mexico	Mexic_____
7 Poland	Pol_____
8 Turkey	Turk_____
9 Russia	Russi_____
10 Vietnam	Vietnam_____

Vocabulary 2
Nationalities (2)

Complete the puzzle.

Across

2 A person from the Czech Republic is _____. (5)

5 A person from France is _____. (6)

6 A person from Poland is _____. (6)

Down

1 A person from Germany is _____. (6)

3 A person from Holland is _____. (5)

4 A person from Thailand is _____. (4)

Where & When

Vocabulary 3A
Describing places

Match the adjectives 1–4 with their opposites a–d.

1	big	a	quiet	———
2	busy	b	noisy	———
3	modern	c	small	———
4	quiet	d	old	———

Vocabulary 3B
Describing places

Complete the sentences with the correct adjective.

1 Rome, in Italy, isn't a modern city. In fact, it's very *noisy / small / old*.

2 Millions of tourists visit Prague in the Czech Republic every year, so it's a *busy / quiet / big* city.

3 Feakle, in Ireland, is normally very *small / quiet / old*, but it's busy during its music festival in August.

4 Milton Keynes, in England, is a new town that was created in the 1960s. It's very *big / modern / quiet*.

5 With its cars, cafés and nightclubs, Madrid, in Spain, is a very *old / noisy / quiet* city.

Extend your vocabulary
also and *too*

Write the second sentence again with *also* or *too*.

1 It's a big city. It's also very noisy.

_____

2 It's a hotel. It's a conference centre too.

_____

3 I'm Spanish. I'm Basque too.

_____

4 We're teachers. We're also students.

_____

5 Biyu and Huilang speak Mandarin. They also speak good English.

_____

6 It's a small town. It's quiet too.

_____

Vocabulary 4A
Daily routine

Complete the expressions with the correct verbs.

1 *go / have / get* breakfast   2 *go / have / get* to work

3 *go / have / get* a meeting   4 *go / have / get* to the gym

5 *go / have / get* dinner

Vocabulary 4B
Daily routine

Complete the description with one word in each gap.

My typical day? Well, I'm a doctor, and I get

(1) _____ at about 7.30 and I

(2) _____ a coffee. Then I have breakfast. I

(3) _____ to work at about 8.15. The hospital's about 2 kilometres from my house, and I

(4) _____ to work at about 8.45. I normally have

(5) _____ at about 2. At 5.30, I

(6) _____ to the gym. I normally get

(7) _____ at 7.30 and go to (8) _____ at midnight.

Where & When

Vocabulary 5
Time

Complete the world records with the words in the box. There is one word you don't need.

seconds	minutes	hours	days	months	years
decades

1 Going around the world on a bicycle – more than 6 _____.

2 Walking around the world – more than 4 _____.

3 Maximum age for humans – more than 12 _____.

4 Running 100 metres – under 10 _____.

5 Swimming 1500 metres – under 15 _____.

6 Running a marathon (40 km) – more than 2 _____.

Vocabulary 6A
Days and months

Complete the sentences with the days and months in the box.

February	Friday	January	Thursday	April
August	December	Tuesday	May	Monday
November	June	July	March	October
Wednesday	Saturday	Sunday	September	

1 The weekend is _____ and _____.

2 In most Western countries, the year starts in _____.

3 The first day after the weekend is _____.

4 October is before _____ and after _____.

5 The day before Thursday is _____.

6 In Europe, the three summer months are June, _____ and _____.

7 The second month in the Gregorian calendar is _____.

8 The tenth month in the Gregorian calendar is _____.

Vocabulary 6B
Days and months

1.05 Listen to the dates and write the day and the month. Remember to use a capital letter at the start of all the words.

1 _____ 10th _____
2 _____ 15th _____
3 _____ 2nd _____
4 _____ 30th _____
5 _____ 3rd _____
6 _____ 21st _____
7 _____ 5th _____

Pronunciation 1
Nationalities

1.06 Listen and choose the correct pronunciation. The underlined syllables are stressed.

1 a Russian b Russian
2 a Italian b Italian c Italian
3 a American b American c American
4 a Chinese b Chinese
5 a Scottish b Scottish
6 a Swedish b Swedish
7 a Vietnamese b Vietnamese c Vietnamese
8 a Japanese b Japanese c Japanese

Pronunciation 2
/s/, /z/, /ɪz/

1.07 Listen and choose the sound you hear for –s or –es. Circle your answers.

1	He gets to work at 8.	/S/	/Z/	/IZ/
2	Here are your keys.	/S/	/Z/	/IZ/
3	She finishes work at 6.	/S/	/Z/	/IZ/
4	He has lunch at work.	/S/	/Z/	/IZ/
5	Three buses go to the centre.	/S/	/Z/	/IZ/
6	Where are my books?	/S/	/Z/	/IZ/
7	These are easy exercises.	/S/	/Z/	/IZ/
8	I remember school dinners.	/S/	/Z/	/IZ/

Where & When

Listening
Global cities

🔊 **1.08** Listen to a radio programme about global cities and complete the fact file. You don't need to use all the words and phrases in the box.

airport	global city	institutions	inhabitants
Johannesburg	megacity	New York	Tokyo
transport	universities		

Global cities fact-file

Definition:

A (1) _____ is important to the world's economy.

The top global cities:

1st (2) _____, London

2nd Beijing, Hong Kong, (3) _____, Paris, Sydney

Essential characteristic of global cities:

International corporations and (4) _____

Other characteristics:

An international (5) _____ and an advanced (6) _____ system

Important (7) _____ and museums

Where & When

Reading
Have a nap

1 Match the words 1–3 with the definitions a–c.

1 nap   _____

2 siesta   _____

3 xiuxi   _____

a a Chinese word for a short sleep after lunch

b a short sleep during the day

c a Spanish word for a short sleep after lunch, also used in English

2 Read the article and *Nap facts* and check your answers to exercise 1.

3 Read the article and *Nap facts* again and answer the questions.

1 Where is a nap after lunch part of the daily routine?

_____

2 What is the first activity after lunch in Chinese schools?

_____

3 Why isn't a siesta common in North America and some European countries?

_____

4 Why is a siesta good for you?

_____

5 How much (in dollars) does a 40-minute nap cost at *Metronaps*?

_____

6 How long is the perfect siesta?

_____

4 Complete the sentences with words or phrases from the article.

1 My children are always _____

_____ energy after school. (Paragraph 1)

2 I go to bed at 10pm. I'm always _____ at 10. (Paragraph 1)

3 Please stop talking. I can't _____ on my work. (Paragraph 4)

4 Microsoft is an _____ of a big American

_____. (Paragraph 5)

5 Complete the text with the present simple form of the verbs in brackets.

Sleep is a big problem today, especially in cities. We
(1) _____ (*need*) to sleep seven or eight hours a night, but many people (2) _____ (*not sleep*) this much. They (3) _____ (*work*) long hours and the day (4) _____ (*not finish*) until late at night. This isn't just bad for you, it can also be dangerous, because a tired person (5) _____ (*have*) more accidents. One solution is a siesta after lunch. A siesta
(6) _____ (*not take*) much time, and you
(7) _____ (*work*) more after a short sleep.

Have a nap

It's a typical day. You get up full of energy. You work or study all morning. You have lunch, and then something changes. You can't concentrate. You feel tired.

In many countries, people have a *siesta* – a nap or short sleep – after lunch. In China it's called *xiuxi*, and schools in China stop for a 30-minute nap after lunch. Some Japanese offices have a special nap room for workers, and a nap is also common in South Asia, North Africa and southern Europe.

In North America and other European countries, a siesta isn't common. People sometimes have a negative opinion of them because if you sleep, you don't work. So people in these places often have a coffee after lunch.

But scientific studies suggest that a siesta is good for you. It gives you more energy, and you can concentrate more. It's better, in fact, than a coffee.

Many companies in the US now think siestas are a good idea, and some have special 'wellness rooms' for workers. Other companies offer a special napping service. One example is *Metronaps* in New York. For fourteen dollars you can have a 20-minute nap. An extra 20 minutes is $9.50.

Nap facts

The perfect siesta is 20 to 30 minutes long.

The word *siesta* comes from Spanish, and the Latin phrase *hora sexta*, meaning 'the sixth hour' after the day starts, or noon.

Where & When

Writing
Describing daily life

Reading

1 Read the text. What type of text is it?

1 an email to a friend in another country

2 a description on a website about daily life in a specific country

3 a news story from an internet newspaper

In the UK, people generally have breakfast at home before work or school, and then they have a coffee or a small snack in the middle of the morning. The working day typically starts at 9 o'clock. Most shops and banks open at this time.

Lunchtime is generally from 12 o'clock to 1.30. A lot of people at work have just half an hour for lunch, so it's typical to have a small lunch at lunchtime and a big dinner in the evening. Shops stay open at lunchtime, and a lot of people buy sandwiches during their lunch break.

School generally finishes at about 4 o'clock, and a lot of people finish work at 5 o'clock. Most shops close at 5.30, but big supermarkets stay open until 8 or 9 o'clock. Banks close between 4.30 and 5 o'clock.

It's typical to have dinner at 6 o'clock. If you go out to eat, or go for a drink after dinner, pubs are generally open until 11pm and a lot of restaurants close at this time, too.

2 Read the description again and complete the table with typical times.

	When?
Breakfast	before work or school
Work	9am – (1) _____
School	9am – (2) _____
Shops	9am – (3) _____
Banks	9am – 4:30 or (4) _____
Lunchtime	12am – (5) _____
Dinner	(6) _____
Pubs and restaurants	until (7) _____

Language focus: prepositions of time

3 Underline the prepositions in the text. Then complete the sentences with the prepositions in the box.

after	at	before	during	from / to	until

1 School generally starts _____ 9am.

2 People normally work _____ 9am _____ 5pm.

3 Most shops are open _____ 5:30.

4 People at work have a break _____ the morning.

5 Banks close _____ shops.

6 People typically have a big meal _____ work.

Writing skills: describing typical routines

4 Complete the phrases with words from the text.

1 People generally / _____ / _____ have / start, etc.

2 It's _____ to have / start, etc.

3 Most / _____ people have / start, etc.

Preparing to write

5 Make notes about when things happen in your country. Use the table in exercise 2 to help you. Organise your notes into four paragraphs:

Paragraph 1:   Before work / school

Paragraph 2:   Lunchtime

Paragraph 3:   In the afternoon

Paragraph 4:   After work / school

Writing

6 You visit an internet site about daily life around the world. Your country isn't included. Write a description for your country. Use your notes and the Useful phrases to help you.

Useful phrases

- *The working / school day typically starts at …*
- *… in the middle of the morning / afternoon.*
- *A lot of people have just half an hour for …*
- *Shops stay open at lunchtime / until 8pm*
- *If you go out to eat / for a drink after dinner …*

Family & Friends

Grammar 1A
Possessive 's

Choose the correct option to complete the sentences.

1 My *brother's / brothers'* wife is from Algeria.
2 Is this your *girlfriend's / girlfriends'* mobile phone?
3 His *cousin's / cousins'* names are Nick and Angela.
4 Her *mother's / mothers'* car has a personalised number plate.
5 We have a meeting at our *children's / childrens'* school today.
6 My *parent's / parents'* birthdays are both on September 1st.

Grammar 1B
Possessive 's

Complete the sentences with the words in brackets and *'s* or *'*.

1 Your _____ is your uncle. (cousin / father)
2 Your _____ are your great-grandparents. (grandparents / parents)
3 Vientiane is _____. (Laos / capital city)
4 My _____ are my cousins. (uncle / children)
5 France is _____ tourist destination. (the world / most popular)
6 My _____ is Melanie. (sister / name)

Grammar 2A
Questions with *do / does*

Complete the questions and answers with the correct form of *do*.

A: (1) *Do / Does* Scotland have its own language?
B: Yes, it (2) *do / does*. It's called Scottish Gaelic.
A: (3) *Do / Does* you speak Scottish Gaelic?
B: Yes, I (4) *do / does*, but not very well.
A: And (5) *do / does* your parents come from Edinburgh?
B: No, they (6) *do / don't*. My parents both come from Aberdeen.
A: One final question. (7) *Do / Does* people think the Loch Ness Monster really exists?
B: (8) No, they *don't / doesn't*. But don't tell the tourists. Loch Ness is a very popular destination!

Grammar 2B
Questions with *do / does*

Complete the questions with the correct form of *do* and the words in brackets.

1 A: _____ any brothers and sisters? (you / have)
   B: Yes, I do. I have a brother. He lives in Australia.
2 A: _____ you a lot? (your brother / visit)
   B: No, he doesn't. Australia's very far from here!
3 A: _____? (both your parents / work)
   B: Yes, they do. They both work at a school.
4 A: _____ a car? (your father / have)
   B: My father has a car, but I don't.
5 A: _____ your father's car sometimes? (you / use)
   B: No, I don't. I can't drive.
6 A: _____ in the same town as you? (your grandparents / live)
   B: No, they don't. They live in the south of England.

Grammar 3A
Wh- questions

Complete the conversation with one word from each column in the table.

What	do	you	ask
Where	does	Tom	do
When		Tom and Greg	get
Why		they	go
			meet

A: (1) _____ their friends?
B: In the park I think.
A: (2) _____ to the park?
B: Because it's near the school, I guess.
A: (3) _____ there?
B: They play basketball.
A: (4) _____ home?
B: At about 7. (5) _____?
A: I ask because Greg gets home at 9 some days.
B: That's because he's in the school basketball team. He has an important match next week, remember.
A: Yes, that's true.

UNIT **3** # Family & Friends

Grammar 3B
Wh- questions

Write questions for the answers.

1 Q: _____
   A: I go shopping at the market.
2 Q: _____
   A: The market opens at 6.
3 Q: _____
   A: People like video games because they're exciting.
4 Q: _____
   A: Mall means shopping centre.
5 Q: _____
   A: People play basketball on a court.
6 Q: _____
   A: February has 29 days in a leap year.

Grammar 4A
Object pronouns

Complete the sentences with the correct object pronouns in the box.

| me | you | him | her | it | us | you | them |

1 I have a sister, but I don't see _____ a lot.
2 I don't know Mr Kameni. Is that _____?
3 Do you like rats? I hate _____.
4 We don't like our new teacher. He doesn't listen to _____.
5 I like Yoko, but she doesn't like _____.
6 Ron? Denis? Where are you? I can't see _____.
7 Vietnam's a beautiful country. We love _____.
8 I'm sorry, Naglaa, but my dog doesn't like _____!

Grammar 4B
Object pronouns

Complete the email with object pronouns.

Hey Tomo! We've got a new pet! His name's Fangs and here's a photo of (1) _____. Yes, he's a spider. A lot of people don't like (2) _____, but spiders are really good pets. Judi isn't very happy because she hates spiders and Fangs is really big, but I think Fangs likes (3) _____. Anyway, why don't you come and see (4) _____ at the weekend? We don't see

(5) _____ a lot, and you can meet Fangs too.

Jaquie and Sal

P.S. Do you have your new car? Do you like (6) _____?

Vocabulary 1A
Family

Put the family words in the box into the correct group.

brother	wife	daughter	father	mother	children
son	sister	aunt	grandfather	husband	uncle
cousin	granddaughter				

Male ♂	Female ♀	Male and female

Vocabulary 1B
Family

Complete the descriptions with the correct family words.

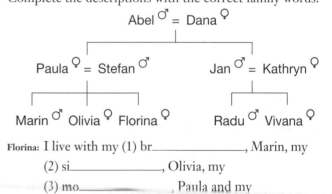

Florina: I live with my (1) br_____, Marin, my
(2) si_____, Olivia, my
(3) mo_____, Paula and my
(4) fa_____, Stefan. My grandfather, Abel, and my (5) gr_____, Dana, live in our house too. I have two (6) co_____ – Radu and Viviana.

Abel: Dana's my (7) wi_____, Paula's my daughter, and Jan's my (8) so_____. Paula and her (9) hu_____, Stefan, have three (10) ch_____ – Marin, Olivia and Florina, and Jan and Kathryn have two – my (11) gr_____ Radu and my (12) gr_____ Viviana.

Family & Friends

Vocabulary 2
Colours

Complete the colours. Look at the clues if you need help.

Colour		Clues
1 b_____		night, space
2 w_____		milk, paper
3 g_____		1+2
4 r_____		Stop! tomatoes, London buses
5 y_____		bananas, a desert, New York taxis
6 o_____		juice, 4+5
7 b_____		the sky, the sea, a lake
8 g_____		Go! trees, forest, 7+5
9 b_____		coffee with milk

Vocabulary 3A
Describing what you do with friends

Match the sentence beginnings with the endings.

1 My friends and I meet _____
2 We normally talk _____
3 On Fridays we sometimes see _____
4 Some weekends we play _____
5 My best friend, Jacoub, lives _____
6 We often go for _____

a five minutes from my house.
b football in the park.
c up at a cafe.
d a film together.
e a walk by the river.
f about our work.

Vocabulary 3B
Describing what you do with friends

Complete the text with the correct words.

'I think boys and girls today have similar opportunities, but we do different things when we meet (1) *about / up / for*. The boys I know (2) *play / play to / have* football. Girls sit and talk (3) *in / at / about* things – and not just sport and music, like boys. Or sometimes we (4) *go to shopping / shopping / go shopping* or we (5) *go / go to / meet* a restaurant, but we always talk (6) *up / about / a lot*. Boys don't generally like shopping. My friends live (7) *in / for / at* the same part of town, so I (8) *see to / see / meet up* my friends every day.

Vocabulary 4A
Adjectives to describe characteristics

Complete the sentences with the opposite of the underlined adjectives. Use the adjectives in the box.

awful   unfriendly   stupid   dirty   ugly

1 Camels aren't <u>beautiful</u>. They're really _____.
2 Some cats are <u>friendly</u>, but your cat's really
   _____.
3 People think rats are _____, but they're really <u>nice</u> pets.
4 And rats aren't _____. In fact, they're very <u>clean</u> animals.
5 Dolphins are very <u>intelligent</u>. People are _____!

Vocabulary 4B
Adjectives to describe characteristics

Complete the adjective in the sentences.

1 People like Uri because he's very f_____.
2 We love Mexican food. It's really n_____.
3 There's a b_____ square in Marrakesh in Morocco.
4 Gigi's the best student in the class. She's very i_____.
5 The Tokyo metro's fantastic. It's really c_____.

Extend your vocabulary
really

Put the words in the correct order to make sentences.

1 cats / I / hate / really / .

_____

2 noisy / is / really / city / this / a / .

_____

3 love / our / really / car / we / .

_____

4 are / parks / beautiful / London's / really / .

_____

5 are / friendly / horses / really / animals / .

_____

6 really / sister / likes / my / shopping / .

_____

Family & Friends

Pronunciation 1
Intonation in questions

🔘 **1.09**

1 Listen and choose the correct intonation in the questions. Does it rise (↗) or fall (↘)? Circle your answers.

1	A: Where are you from?	↗ | ↘
	B: I'm from Milan in Italy.	
2	A: What's Milan like?	↗ | ↘
	B: It's very big.	
3	A: Do you have a big family?	↗ | ↘
	B: Yes, I do.	
4	A: Are you married?	↗ | ↘
	B: Yes, I am.	
5	A: What's your husband's name?	↗ | ↘
	B: Mehmet.	
6	A: Does he come from Italy?	↗ | ↘
	B: No, he doesn't. He's Turkish.	
7	A: Do you live in Milan now?	↗ | ↘
	B: No we don't. We live in Turkey.	

2 Choose the correct option to complete the rule.

Intonation rises in *Yes/No questions / Wh-questions*.

Pronunciation 2
Emphasising

🔘 **1.10** Listen and choose the correct verb.

1 A: Does Marcus like football?
 B: Football? He *loves / likes / hates* it.
2 A: Do you like rap music?
 B: Rap music? I *love / like / hate* it.
3 A: What do you think of dogs?
 B: Dogs? I *love / like / hate* them.
4 A: Does Myrna like coffee?
 B: Coffee? She *loves / likes / hates* it.
5 A: What's your opinion of shopping?
 B: Shopping? I *love / like / hate* it.
6 A: Do your grandparents like computers?
 B: Computers? They *love / like / hate* them.

2 Listen again. Which word in the answers is stressed?

a The verb (*love, like, hate*)
b The object pronoun (*it, they*)

Listening
Interviews at a music festival

🔘 **1.11** Listen to three people at a music festival. Which person or people say these things?

		Jo	Misha	Yara
1	He/She meets friends at the festival.			
2	He/She is in one of the groups at the festival.			
3	She/He is at the festival with children.			
4	It's his/her first visit to the festival.			
5	She/He likes music from different countries.			
6	He/She thinks the festival is noisy at night.			

Family & Friends

Reading
How many friends?

1 What's the ideal number of good friends? Write your answer. Then read the blog and write the blog's answer.

1 My answer: _____

2 The blog's answer: _____

2 Read the blog again. Complete the questions and answers with words from the blog.

1 What type of site is Facebook?

It's a _____ site.

2 What does Robin Dunbar do?

He's an _____.

3 What's his definition of a _____?

It's a person you know, and you also know their

_____.

4 What does Patrick think of Dunbar's _____?

He thinks it's a lot of people, but he thinks it's

_____.

5 Does Patrick have time to _____?

No, he doesn't!

3 Write a sentence about these numbers in the blog. Include the numbers in the sentences.

1 200 million

_____

2 120

_____

3 150

_____

4 Find words and phrases in the blog to match these definitions.

1 You know these people, but they aren't good friends. (Paragraph 2)

_____

2 In the opinion of (Paragraph 3)

_____

3 good (to describe a friend) (Paragraph 5)

_____

4 In my opinion, that's more or less correct. (Paragraph 6)

_____

5 Complete the text with object pronouns.

Today, more and more people use social networking sites. We use (1) _____ because they help (2) _____ to make friends and stay in contact with (3) _____. They are particularly good for old people. I'm 75 and I can't walk now. Also, my daughter lives in another country, and I don't see (4) _____ a lot. But my friends and my family can contact (5) _____ at my MyWay page. I visit (6) _____ every day to read my new messages.

How many friends?

By Patrick Prevatt

Social networking sites are changing the way we make and communicate with friends. More than 200 million people now use *Facebook*, and the site says its users have about 120 friends.

When I read that, my first question was, is 120 a typical number? How many good friends do people have, and how many are really just acquaintances? And what's the *ideal* number of friends?

According to Robin Dunbar, a British anthropologist, there's a maximum number of friends a person can have. His definition of a friend is that you know the person and their place in your social world. In anthropology it's called Dunbar's number. The figure isn't exact, but it's about 150.

'That's a lot of people', was my first reaction. But I look in my address book … friends from school, from university, at work … and I see it's possible. And, of course, not all these friends have the same importance. Do you have time to meet 150 friends regularly? I don't! These people are in my social world, but they aren't *good* friends.

Dunbar categorises the 150 people into four different groups or circles. In the centre, we have five very close friends. The next circle adds ten more people, the next 35, and the final circle adds 100.

So, the ideal number of best friends is five, with about another ten good friends. That seems about right to me!

Family & Friends

Writing
Describing people

Reading

1 Read the email and complete the sentences.

1 James is Nick's _____.

2 Elsie and Kevin are Nick's _____ and _____.

3 Tom and Barbara are Nick's _____.

Hi James,

How are you? I'm writing because my aunt's on holiday in Italy with her family. They want to spend next weekend in Sant'Agnello. Do you have time to meet them and give them some suggestions – things to do, places to eat, etc.?

My aunt's name's Elsie and her husband's name's Kevin. They both like quiet places and going for walks and I think Sant'Agnello's the perfect place for them. They have two children called Tom and Barbara. They're teenagers but they're both very friendly. He likes computers and chatting online. Does the town have an internet café? She likes football. Is it easy to get to Naples to see a football match? They all like going to the beach. Does Sant'Agnello have any good beaches? And they all love Italian food!

Thanks for any help you can give, and don't worry if you can't meet them.

All the best

Nick

---

2 Read the email again and write the names of the people.

1 _____ lives in Sant'Agnello.

2 _____ need some suggestions.

3 _____ like going for walks.

4 _____ are very friendly.

5 _____ like going to the beach.

6 _____ like Italian food.

Language focus: *both* and *all*

3 Look at the examples and the explanations. Then write the sentences again with *both* or *all*.

They're both very friendly.
They all love Italian food!

Both refers to two people or things.

All refers to three or more people or things.

Both and *all* come after *be* and before other verbs.

1 Elsie and Tom like football.
They _____.

2 Elsie, Kevin and their children are on holiday.
They _____.

3 James and his friends stay in touch by email.
They _____.

4 Tom and Barbara go to school in Glasgow.
They _____.

Preparing to write

4 Imagine you have a friend in another part of the world. A family you know wants to visit his/her town. You are going to write an email to your friend. First, make notes for the two paragraphs of your email.

Paragraph 1:

Say why you are writing

Introduce the family and the help they need

Paragraph 2:

Describe the family members and their interests

Ask your friend questions about where they live

Writing

Write your email. Use your notes and the Useful phrases to help you.

> ### Useful phrases
>
> - *I'm writing because …*
> - *Do you know of a / any … ?*
> - *Do you have time to …?*
> - *Is it easy to get to / find / buy … ?*
> - *Thanks for any help you can give / suggestions you have.*
> - *Don't worry if you can't …*

Grammar 1A
There is / There are

Complete the description with *is, isn't, are* and *aren't*.

The Hotel Chelsea in New York is famous. It's well-known for its guests – artists, musicians and writers – and there (1) _____ examples of their work on the walls.

There (2) _____ different types of rooms at the hotel, with different facilities. There (3) _____ cable television in all rooms, but there (4) _____ a bath in every room – some rooms share a bath with another room.

It's an old hotel, so there (5) _____ a swimming pool and there (6) _____ any facilities for business people, for example a meeting room. But it's in the centre of New York, and it's an interesting place to stay.

Grammar 1B
There is / There are

Complete the conversation with the correct form of *there is* and *there are*.

A: World Star Hotel, how can I help you?

B: I'd like some information about the hotel. For example, (1) *there is / there are / is there* a heated swimming pool?

A: Yes, (2) *there is / there are / is there*. There's a heated pool indoors, and a cold pool outdoors.

B: (3) *Is there / Are there / There are* good views of the sea?

A: (4) Yes, *there aren't / there are / are there*. All rooms have sea views.

B: (5) *There is / Is there / Are there* a gym?

A: (6) No, *isn't there / there isn't / there aren't*, I'm afraid.

B: (7) *Are there / There are / There aren't* any guided tours for us to go on?

A: Yes. (8) *There is / There are / Are there* guided tours of the city every day.

B: Great. I'd like to make a reservation.

Grammar 2A
Countable and uncountable nouns

Complete the shopping list with *a, an* or *some*.

Shopping list
(1) *a / some* eggs
(2) *an / some* apple
(3) *a / some* coffee
(4) *a / some* biscuits
(5) *an / some* orange
(6) *a / some* fruit juice
(7) *a / some* bread
(8) *a / some* banana

Grammar 2B
Countable and uncountable nouns

Are these sentences correct or incorrect? Tick (✔) your answers.

		correct	incorrect
1	I'd like an orange juice with my breakfast.		
2	We have a bread and butter with our lunch.		
3	There are some bananas in the fridge.		
4	Would you like a cup of coffee?		
5	We take an apples to work.		
6	I normally have a toast and jam for breakfast.		
7	Please buy some eggs at the market.		
8	My grandfather eats a fruit for breakfast.		

Bed & Breakfast

Grammar 3A
Quantifiers (a lot of, much, many, some)

Complete the description with the correct quantifiers.

The Mediterranean diet

The Mediterranean diet is famous around the world because it's very good for you. Traditionally, people in this area eat (1) *a lot of / much* fruit and vegetables, and they don't eat (2) *much / many* chips. In fact, they don't eat (3) *much / many* processed food at all. They eat (4) *a / some* fish and (5) *a / some* cheese, but they don't eat (6) *much / many* meat and don't eat (7) *much / many* eggs. They usually eat (8) *a / some* rice, potatoes or pasta with meals.

Grammar 3B
Quantifiers (a lot of, much, many, some)

Complete the description with *a lot of, some, not much, not many* and the verbs in brackets.

'At home we (1) _____ (*eat*) fruit because we don't like it, but we (2) _____ (*have*) vegetables – about five different types every day. I'm a vegetarian and I don't eat meat, but my wife (3) _____ (*cook*) meat, maybe two or three days a week.

At work it's a different story. The company restaurant (4) _____ (*prepare*) fresh food – a lot of it is processed. There (5) _____ (*be*) things I like, so I (6) _____ (*eat*) pizzas – three or four a week!

Vocabulary 1A
Hotel facilities

Match the sentence beginnings to the endings.

1	There's a car	a	transfer for all its guests.
2	There's a swimming	b	park under the hotel.
3	You can go on guided	c	room for business customers.
4	The hotel offers airport	d	restaurant and gym.
5	There's internet	e	television in all rooms.
6	There's a meeting	f	pool behind the hotel.
7	You can watch cable	g	tours from the hotel.
8	The hotel also has a bar,	h	access in all rooms.

Vocabulary 1B
Hotel facilities

Complete the words in the description of a hotel.

TOP HOTEL

Stay at a Top Hotel. Here are just some of the advantages!

You don't need a taxi to the airport. We offer free airport (1) t_____.

Leave your car in our free car (2) p_____.

Meet to talk about business in our meeting (3) r_____.

Go online and check emails with our free internet (4) a_____.

Exercise in our (5) g_____ or swim in our swimming (6) p_____.

Relax with a drink in our (7) b_____.

Eat local and international food in our (8) r_____.

Visit the sights of the city with our guided (9) t_____.

Watch your favourite programmes on (10) c_____ television.

Vocabulary 2A
Furniture

Put the furniture in the correct category.

bath	cooker	couch/sofa	cupboard	fridge
lamp	armchair	shelf	shower	toilet	wardrobe

Kitchen	Living room	Bathroom	Bedroom	Two or more rooms

Vocabulary 2B
Furniture

Complete the words.

In the bathroom, we have ...

1 a ba_____.

2 a sh_____.

3 a to_____.

In the kitchen, there is ...

4 a co_____.

5 a fr_____.

6 a cu_____.

In the living room, we have ...

7 an ar_____.

8 a co_____ or so_____.

9 a sh_____.

In the bedroom, there is ...

10 a wa_____.

11 a la_____.

Vocabulary 3A
Food and drink

Put the food and drink in the correct category.

| fish   rice   cheese   bread   jam   milk   oranges |
| butter   cakes   eggs   bananas   juice   a cup of tea |
| coffee |

Dairy products	Drinks	Fruit	Other things

Vocabulary 3B
Food and drink

Complete the food and drink words.

1 f_____   2 r_____

3 j_____   4 c_____

5 ch_____   6 m_____

Extend your vocabulary
a type of, a kind of, a sort of

Put the words in the correct order to make sentences.

1 type / tea / is / a / Darjeeling / of / .

_____

2 of / Marmalade / a / sort / is / jam / .

_____

3 is /a / of / kind / Cappuccino / coffee/ .

_____

4 A / is / kind / dictionary /of / book/ a / .

_____

5 are / Motels / a / hotel / sort / of /.

_____

6 transport / A / is / a / of / taxi / type / .

_____

Bed & Breakfast

Vocabulary 4
Fresh food & processed food

Complete the puzzle.

Across

2 It's white or brown and people eat it around the world. (4)

5 They're made from potatoes. They come in a packet. (6)

7 They're a red vegetable. (8)

8 They're an orange vegetable. (7)

9 They're a green vegetable. (5)

Down

1 The word for this food is Italian. (5)

3 They're called French fries in US English. (5)

4 We eat the _____ of different animals. (4)

6 They're a brown vegetable that is white inside. (8)

Pronunciation 1
Consonant clusters

1.12 Listen and complete the words with two or three consonants.

1 Is this your gra____ather's house?

2 His dog's very frie____y.

3 Does it sleep ou____oors in the ____uare?

4 Is there a la____ in this room?

5 There's one on the she____ near that ar____air.

6 There's a ____idge in his ba____oom!

Pronunciation 2
Linking words

1.13 Listen and underline the pairs of linked words in each sentence. In some sentences there are two pairs of linked words.

1 Camel's milk is very nice.

2 Feta? It's a sort of cheese.

3 Brownies are cakes.

4 Ciabatta is a type of bread.

5 Fish is good for you.

6 Does Rajiv want a cup of tea?

7 Basmati? It's a kind of rice.

8 Do the children want a glass of milk?

Listening
A home exchange

1.14 Listen to the phone conversation about a home exchange and choose the correct answers.

1 Where is the village?
   a It's near the sea.
   b It's near the mountains.
   c It's near a train station.

2 What's the village like in July and August?
   a It's busy.
   b It's noisy.
   c It's quiet.

3 Where's the supermarket?
   a In the village.
   b 15 minutes from the house.
   c 50 minutes from the house.

4 What's the best way to get to the house?
   a On a bus – there are a lot of buses.
   b In a taxi.
   c On foot – you can walk from the station.

5 What facilities does the house have?
   a An internet connection and cable TV.
   b An internet connection but no cable TV.
   c Cable TV but no internet connection.

6 What things are there for children?
   a There's a park in the village, but there aren't any other things.
   b There are TV programmes for children.
   c There are a lot of things in the house for children.

Bed & Breakfast

Reading
The vegetarian option

1 Are these sentences true (*T*) or false (*F*)? Circle your answers.

1 Vegetarians don't eat any meat	*T / F*
2 70% of people in India don't eat any meat.	*T / F*
3 Eating a lot of meat is bad for our planet.	*T / F*
4 People eat vegetarian food around the world.	*T / F*

2 Read the magazine article and check your answers to exercise 1.

The vegetarian option

In today's food column, we look at vegetarian food. It's a popular option in restaurants around the world, but what exactly is a vegetarian?

Vegetarians, semi-vegetarians and vegans

Vegetarians don't eat any meat or fish. That is clear, but there are different types of vegetarian. Vegans, for example, don't eat any animal products, so vegan food doesn't have any cheese, eggs or milk in it. Other people are semi-vegetarians and eat some fish but don't eat any meat.

Why be a vegetarian?

About 70% of the world's vegetarians live in India, where about 30% of the population are vegetarians. A lot of these people are Hindus, so religion is an important reason for eating vegetarian food.

Other people eat vegetarian food to help our planet. We eat a lot of meat, and to make the space to produce it, we need to cut down trees and plants, and that's bad for the environment. Also, to produce 1 kilo of meat, an animal needs 8 kilos of vegetarian food. It's better for the global population if *we* eat this food.

There are also vegetarians who think it's wrong to eat animals, or who eat vegetarian food because it's healthy.

A global option

For all these reasons, vegetarian food has a good future. Between 3 and 7% of people in the UK are vegetarian, and 86% of the population eat vegetarian food one or two days a week. In Brazil the figure is between 5 and 10%. And Ghent, in Belgium, is the first city in the world to have one official vegetarian day every week.

Glossary

cut down (*verb*) – to make a tree fall to the ground

Hindu (*noun*) – a person who follows Hinduism, the major religion in India

produce (*verb*) – to make or grow

religion (*noun*) – Hinduism, Islam, Buddhism and Christianity are examples of a religion

wrong (*adjective*) – bad, not good

Bed & Breakfast

3 Complete the table with Yes and No.

	What do they eat?		
	Meat	Fish	Cheese and eggs
Semi-vegetarians			
Vegetarians			
Vegans			

4 Complete the questions with the correct option. Then answer the questions.

1 How *much / many* reasons does the article mention for eating vegetarian food?

_____

2 How *much / many* food does an animal eat to produce a kilo of meat?

_____

3 How *much / many* people in the UK are vegetarians?

_____

4 How *much / often* does Ghent have a vegetarian day?

_____

5 Complete the description with *any, some, much, many* or *a lot of*.

December 4, 2008

FLEXITARIAN, NOT VEGETARIAN

'I'm a flexitarian. I'm not a vegetarian, but I don't eat (1) _____ meat, just one or two times a week. I eat (2) _____ vegetarian food – two or three times a day – , and I also eat (3) _____ fish for lunch or dinner two days a week. I don't eat (4) _____ fruit because I hate it.

I don't have (5) _____ reasons for being a flexitarian – just one, in fact. Vegetarian food is good for the planet. There are (6) _____ people in the world who need more food – millions of people – and vegetarian food is more economical to produce.

Writing
Asking for more information
Reading

1 Match the email below with description a or b.

a

Holiday apartment to rent in Mykonos. Self-catering (no meals provided) or half board (breakfast and dinner provided). Near the beach. For more information, contact …

b

Big holiday apartment to rent near the centre of Athens. Self-catering (no meals provided). For more information, contact …

Dear Talia

I'd like some more information about the holiday apartment to rent.

The description says it's a big apartment. We're a group of five friends. How big is it? How many bedrooms are there? Could you send us a photo of the rooms?

The description also says the apartment is near the city centre. How far from the centre is it? Can we walk there? If not, are there buses? Could you send me the address?

Another question is about food. The apartment is self-catering. Does it have a fridge? And is there a supermarket near the apartment?

Finally, I'd like to know about the price and when it's available. We'd like to rent it in the first or second week of July. Is it available for one of those weeks? And how much does it cost for 7 days?

I look forward to hearing from you.

Best wishes,

Karim

Bed & Breakfast

2 Look at Karim's list. Tick (✔) the things he asks about in his email.

Holiday apartment list

Number of bedrooms? _____
Big kitchen? _____
Near centre? _____
Buses? _____
Address? _____
Telephone number? _____
Price? _____
When available? _____
How to pay? _____

Language focus: questions

3 Complete the questions with *are/is, do/does* or *could*. Remember that we use *could* for requests.

1 _____ the rooms very big?

2 _____ you confirm our reservation?

3 _____ the bedrooms all have double beds?

4 _____ there a swimming pool near the apartment?

5 _____ the apartment have a terrace?

6 _____ you give me your mobile number?

4 Complete questions 1–4 with one word. Read the email to check. Then match the questions with a–d.

1 _____ big is it? _____

2 _____ many beds are there? _____

3 _____ far is it from the beach? _____

4 _____ much does it cost for a weekend? _____

a I want to know the number.
b I want to know the price.
c I want to know the size (big or small).
d I want to know the distance (near or far).

Preparing to write

5 Imagine you are going on holiday. Prepare a list of things to ask about apartment a in exercise 1. Use the list in exercise 2 to help you.

Writing

Write an email asking for more information about apartment a in exercise 1, or about another holiday apartment. Use your notes and the Useful phrases to help you.

Useful phrases

- *The description (also) says …*
- *Another question is about …*
- *Can we walk / use / etc. … ? If not, …?*
- *Finally, I'd like to know about …*
- *Is it available …?*
- *I look forward to hearing from you.*
- *Best wishes,*

Grammar 1A
Frequency adverbs (*every day / week / month*)

Match the frequency expressions 1–6 with a–f.

1 every two weeks _____
2 on Monday, Thursday and Friday _____
3 at 8am and 8pm _____
4 every twelve months _____
5 in January, June, September and December _____
6 every two days _____

a once a year
b four times a year
c three or four times a week
d three times a week
e twice a month
f twice a day

Grammar 1B
Frequency adverbs (*every day / week / month*)

Put the words in the correct order to make sentences.

A: Can I ask you some questions about your cinema habits?
B: Sure.
A: How often do you go to the cinema?
B: (1) month / to the cinema / We / three times / go / a / .

_____

A: OK. And how often do you watch films on TV?
B: (2) every / watch / two days / a film on TV / We / .

_____

A: And how often do you watch DVDs?
B: (3) a / about / twice / We / DVDs / month / watch / .

_____

A: What about the internet? How often do you download films from the internet?
B: (4) We / week / a film / every / download / .

_____

A: How often do you read film reviews?
B: (5) read / times / I / film reviews / a / week / four or five / .

_____

I love film reviews!
C: (6) I / once / about / year / them / read / a / .

_____

I prefer to be surprised at the cinema.

Grammar 2A
Frequency adverbs (*always, often, sometimes ...*)

Put the frequency adverbs in the correct position on the diagram.

often	sometimes	never	not often	always

_____ often _____ _____ _____

Grammar 2B
Frequency adverbs (always, often, sometimes ...)

Rewrite the sentences with the frequency adverbs in brackets.

1 I don't watch television. (often)

_____

2 There are sports programmes on, and I hate sport! (always)

_____

3 I watch films, but only once or twice a week. (sometimes)

_____

4 I am at home when my favourite programmes are on. (never)

_____

5 I read about interesting documentaries in the TV guide. (often)

_____

6 But they are on late at night. (often)

_____

7 I get up very early. (always)

_____

8 I stay up late to watch a documentary, though. (sometimes)

_____

Film & Television

Grammar 2C
Frequency adverbs (*always*, *often*, *sometimes ...*)

Rewrite the sentences with *always*, *often*, *sometimes*, *not often* or *never*.

1 We watch the news every day.

_____

2 Tom watches football once a week.

_____

3 We buy a newspaper three or four days a week.

_____

4 I cycle to work when the weather is nice.

_____

5 I am home at five o'clock four days a week.

_____

6 There are good programmes on TV after work every day.

_____

7 I don't watch television. I don't have a TV.

_____

Vocabulary 1
A trip to the cinema (1)

Complete the expressions with the correct word.

1 see what's *in / on*
2 read a film *ticket / review*
3 go to the *cinema / film*
4 buy a cinema *ticket / review*
5 watch the *cinema / film*
6 sit *in / at* the *middle / back*
7 sit *in / at* the *middle / back*

Vocabulary 2
A trip to the cinema (2)

Complete the description with the correct verb.

'I love going to the cinema. A typical trip goes like this. First, I look in an online newspaper to
(1) _____ what's on. Then I (2) _____ the reviews for every film. I choose a film and then I
(3) _____ a ticket on the internet. When Saturday comes, I (4) _____ to the cinema. I always (5) _____ at the back when I
(6) _____ a film at the cinema.'

Vocabulary 3A
Types of film

Complete the descriptions with the types of film in the box.

science fiction   thriller   cartoon   horror
romantic drama

1 It's really scary! It's a _____.
2 It made me cry, but it had a happy ending. It was a _____.
3 It was exciting from the start to the finish. It was a _____.
4 It's about a spaceship that goes to another planet. It's a _____.
5 It's very funny and the drawings are fantastic! It's a _____.

Vocabulary 3B
Types of film

Match the sentences 1–5 to a–e.

1 *Toy Story* is my favourite cartoon.   _____
2 *The Bourne Identity* is my favourite thriller.   _____
3 *2001: A Space Odyssey* is my favourite science fiction film.   _____
4 Alfred Hitchcock's *Psycho* is my favourite horror film.   _____
5 And *Slumdog Millionaire* is my favourite romantic drama.   _____

a It's really exciting.
b It's really scary.
c It's really funny for children and adults.
d Some parts of the story are really sad.
e Its vision of the future is very interesting.

Film & Television

Vocabulary 4
Television programmes

Complete the television programmes with the words in the box.

| comedy show | sports programme | TV series |
| documentary | the news | film |

18:00 Real World

This week's (1) _____ is about Japan and Japanese food.

18:30 Bat and Ball

Today's (2) _____ includes cricket from Pakistan and football from Africa.

20:00 The Hotel

More funny situations from this popular

(3) _____

20:30 Friends & family

Today, on the popular (4) _____ Bashir starts a new job, but his mother isn't happy. Watch to find out why.

21:00 The world at 9

Haifa Khosa presents (5) _____ from around the world.

21:45 Cinema ticket

Another opportunity to see Akira Kurosawa's

(6) _____ *Roshomon*.

Vocabulary 5A
Phrasal verbs

Complete the text with the correct words.

Think about other people!

Stand (1) *down / off / up* on a bus or train when an old person needs to sit (2) *down / off / up* in your place.

Turn (3) *down / off / up* your MP 3 player when you're on public transport. Other people don't want to listen too!

Turn (4) *down / off / up* your mobile phone at the cinema or theatre. It's important to be quiet.

Don't turn (5) *down / off / up* your music late at night. Other people need to sleep!

Vocabulary 5B
Phrasal verbs

Complete the conversations with a word from each box.

| Sit | stand | turn |

| down | off | up |

A: Is that the news?

B: Yes, it is.

A: Can you (1) _____ the TV? I can't hear it.

A: Kylie, can you (2) _____ for a moment?

B: Why?

A: I want to see your new jeans. I can't see them if you're on the sofa.

B: OK. What do you think?

A: They're really nice. OK, you can (3) _____ now!

A: Mansour, can you (4) _____ your radio? I can't work.

B: But I want to hear the news.

A: OK. Can you (5) _____ the radio, please?

B: Sure. No problem.

Extend your vocabulary
see, watch

Complete the description with *see* and *watch*.

There are great views from this balcony. I can (1) _____ the city and the sea. Sometimes I sit here for hours and (2) _____ people in the streets down there. People play basketball in that park, and I often (3) _____ their games. And can you (4) _____ that big building? It's a hotel. The people in the top rooms can (5) _____ this balcony. It's funny, because I do exercise here every morning, and sometimes the people in the hotel (6) _____ me!

Film & Television

Pronunciation 1
/ɪ/ and /iː/

🔊 **1.15** Listen and circle the word you hear.

/ɪ/	/iː/
1 rich	reach
2 live	leave
3 still	steal
4 live	leave
5 it	eat
6 his	he's
7 it	eat
8 his	he's
9 rich	reach
10 still	steal

Pronunciation 2
Phrasal verbs

🔊 **1.16** Underline *down*, *off* and *up* if they are stressed.

1 Can you turn up the radio?
2 Please sit down.
3 Don't turn off the computer!
4 We stand up when the teacher comes in.
5 Turn down that TV!
6 Sit down and listen to me.
7 Turn off the television. It's time to go to bed.

Listening
Do you like Hollywood films?

🔊 **1.17** Listen to the radio programme about films. Are the sentences true (*T*) or false (*F*)? Circle your answers.

1 Mei often watches Hollywood films. *T / F*
2 She likes independent films. *T / F*
3 She thinks you can learn things from world cinema. *T / F*
4 She doesn't like watching films in other languages. *T / F*
5 Jason thinks some Hollywood films are sad. *T / F*
6 Mei thinks Hollywood films have new ideas. *T / F*
7 Mei doesn't like the Hollywood version of Vanilla Sky. *T / F*
8 Jason likes seeing his favourite actors in films. *T / F*

UNIT 5 — **Film & Television**

Reading
Global soaps

1 What is a soap opera?

1 a music programme on TV
2 a TV drama series
3 a type of documentary

2 Read the article about soap operas and check your answer to exercise 1. Where are soap operas popular?

Soap operas are popular in

_____

3 Read the article again and complete the notes.

> On the (1) _____ first.
>
> Money to produce them from (2) _____
>
> First soaps in (3) _____ in
> (4) _____
>
> Two types of soap opera – (5) _____
> and _____
>
> In South America, called (6) _____

4 Are these sentences true (*T*) or false (*F*)? Circle your answers.

1 Today's soap operas are very different.   *T / F*
2 You can often watch soap operas every day.   *T / F*
3 Episodes are about the same group of people.   *T / F*
4 Episodes always start a new story.   *T / F*
5 People always watch soaps from the US and
  UK in English.   *T / F*
6 We like soaps because they help us with
  our problems.   *T / F*

5 Soap operas have two world records. What are they?

1 _____
2 _____

6 Match the words from the article with their opposites.

1 first   a complete
2 the same   b continue
3 incomplete   c different
4 finish   d open
5 closed   e last

7 Complete the description with the frequency words and expressions in the box.

> always   four days a week   often   once a year
> sometimes

One of the UK's most popular soaps is *EastEnders*. Millions of people watch it (1) _____, and if you don't see an episode, you can (2) _____ watch it again later the same night. There is a special programme (3) _____, on Christmas Day. It's normally very exciting. As for the actors, a new actor (4) _____ plays the same character, but this doesn't happen very (5) _____.

Film & Television

Global soaps

Hundreds of millions of people around the globe watch them. This makes them the world's most popular type of TV programme. How much do *you* know about soaps?

In the beginning

They were on the radio first – drama series you listened to in daily episodes. They were extremely popular and because the money to produce them was from soap manufacturers, the media called them *soap operas* or *soaps*.

The format

Their basic format is the same today as it was when the first soaps started in the US in the 1930s. Soaps are often on every day and are about the daily lives of people in a particular community or situation. Episodes always finish with a 'cliff-hanger' – an incomplete story that makes you want to see the next episode. Some are 'closed' and finish with an exciting last episode. Others are 'open' and continue for years or decades. *Guiding Light*, one of the first soaps, is still on US TV today and is the world's longest story.

Who watches soaps?

A lot of the world's soaps are in English and Spanish. The US, UK and Australia all produce soaps in English, and these are translated into other languages too. Many Spanish soaps come from South America. They are called *telenovelas*, and are also popular in Spain. People watch soaps in other parts of Europe, too, and in Asia and the Arab world, where Turkish soaps are popular.

Why do we watch them?

Some people say they help us to forget the problems in our daily lives. Others think we use the problems in soaps to help us to talk about our problems. Whatever the answer, soaps really are a global phenomenon.

> **Glossary**
>
> **episode** (*noun*) – one programme in a TV series
>
> **format** (*noun*) – the form that a television programme is produced in
>
> **manufacturer** (*noun*) – a company that makes (manufactures) things
>
> **the media** (*noun*) – newspapers, television and radio
>
> **produce** (*verb*) – plan and make something
>
> **soap** (*noun*) – you use soap to clean your body and your clothes

Film & Television

Writing
Recommending a TV programme

Reading

1 Read the information on a website and answer the questions.

1 Is it an old or a new programme?

_____

2 How often is it on TV?

_____

3 Where is Cicely?

_____

4 What's Ed's ambition?

_____

5 Why does the writer recommend the programme?

_____

○ ○ ○

The Real Entertainment Site

The programmes that real people recommend

Category: TV programmes

Starting next Monday, we can watch all of the TV series Northern Exposure again. It's on Channel 4 at 11pm every night. It's set in a town called Cicely, in Alaska, and it's about a doctor called Joel Fleischman. Joel's from New York, and he hates Cicely. It's small and quiet and he thinks it's really boring. But he learns to like some things about it.

The other main character in the programme is Maggie. At first, Joel doesn't like her, but they become good friends. But they are very different and they often disagree. Another good character is Ed. He loves films and wants to be a film director.

Some people think it's a bit boring, but I recommend it because the characters are all very interesting and you learn a lot about people and life. It's not a comedy, but sometimes it's quite funny.

Describing a TV programme

2 Match the words and phrases in the box to the correct parts of the sentences.

| name of character   place   TV channel   time |
| people and situation |

1 It's on Channel 4 (_____) at 11pm
   (_____).
2 It's set in a town called Cicely (_____).
3 It's about a doctor from New York. He hates Cicely because it's small and quiet (_____).
4 The other main character is Maggie (_____).

Language focus: *quite* and *very*

3 Look at the words in the box. Then choose the correct words to describe the programme. Read the information in exercise 1 again to check your answers.

−		+
quite sad	sad	very sad
a little sad		really sad

1 Joel thinks Cicely is *a little / really* boring.
2 Some people think the programme's *a little / very* boring.
3 The characters are *quite / very* interesting.
4 It's *quite / really* funny.

Preparing to write

4 Make notes about a TV programme you want to recommend. Use the expressions in exercise 2 to help you, and say why you recommend it.

Writing

Write a description of a TV programme for the Real Entertainment Site. Use your notes and the Useful phrases to help you.

Useful phrases

- *The setting is …*
- *Another good character is …*
- *Some people think it's …*
- *I recommend it because …*

Work & Study

Grammar 1A
Can (possibility)

Look at the notes and complete the telephone message with *can* or *can't*.

> Job benefits:
>
> company car ✘
>
> long holidays ✘
>
> professional training ✔
>
> start and finish late some days ✔
>
> free meals ✘
>
> walk to work ✔

'Hi Karim. I have some good news. I got the job! I'm really happy. I (1) _____ use a company car, and I (2) _____ have long holidays in the first two or three years, but I (3) _____ get professional training, and the office is near my house and I (4) _____ walk to work. I (5) _____ start and finish late some days too, but there are no free meals, so I (6) _____ eat for free at work. But I can prepare food at home to take, so that's not a problem.'

Grammar 1B
Can (possibility)

Choose the correct option to complete the conversation.

A: Hey! Svetlana got the job!

B: Really? That's good news. (1) *She can use / Can she use / Can she uses* a company car?

A: No, (2) *she can / can't / she can't*. But she (3) *can walk / cans walk / can to walk* to work, so that's not a problem.

B: And (4) *she can to make / she cans make / can she make* personal phone calls from work?

A: Yes, (5) *she can / she does can / she cans*.

B: Fantastic! Because I (6) *don't can phone / can't phone / can't to phone* her from my job.

A: And (7) *we can go / can we to go / can we go* on holiday this summer?

B: No, (8) *we can / we can't / can't we*! She only has short holidays this year.

Grammar 2
Can (ability)

Complete the job interview with *can* or *can't* and the words in brackets.

A: Good, Mr Golding. I just need to ask you one or two questions. (1) _____ (*you / type*) well?

B: Yes, I (2) _____. I (3) _____ (*type*) 100 words a minute.

A: Excellent! (4) _____ (*you / speak*) Chinese?

B: No, I (5) _____.

A: OK.

B: (6) _____ (*I / ask*) a question about the company?

A: Of course.

B: (7) _____ (*you / give*) me professional training, including languages?

A: Yes, we (8) _____. In fact, we want the new person to learn new skills.

Grammar 3A
Adverbs

Complete the interview with the correct form – the adjective or the adverb.

Tom: Your English is very (1) *good / well*.

Katana: Thank you. I can speak Russian (2) *good / well* too.

Tom: Really? Russian isn't an (3) *easy / easily* language.

Katana: No, but I like languages. I learn (4) *quick / quickly*.

Tom: Can you type (5) *quick / quickly*?

Katana: I'm a little (6) *slow / slowly* – but I can practise!

Grammar 3B
Adverbs

Complete the conversation with the adverb form of the adjectives in brackets.

Tom: I think Katana's perfect for the job. She speaks three European languages (1) _____ (*perfect*), and she can use a computer (2) _____ (*good*). She needs to work in a team, and I think she can work (3) _____ (*easy*) with other people. On the negative side, she types (4) _____ (*bad*). Also, her English is good, but she talks (5) _____ (*slow*). But I don't think those things are problems.

Work & Study

Sandra: Great. Let's offer her the job (6) _____ (*quick*), before she decides to find another one!

Grammar 4A
was / were

Complete the text with the correct options.

Which is the world's oldest university?

The answer is difficult. Many people think that the first universities (1) *was / were* European. The most famous university in Europe is possibly Oxford University, in England. It's not clear when Oxford was founded, but there (2) *was / were* students there in 1096. But Oxford (3) *wasn't / weren't* the first university in Europe. The first (4) *was / were* the University of Bologna in Italy, founded in 1088.

However, there (5) *was / were* centres of advanced learning in Africa and Asia a long time before that. They (6) *wasn't / weren't* exactly the same as universities in Europe, but they (7) *was / were* equally important. There (8) *was / were* a university in Nalanda in India in the fifth century BC, but it closed in the 1100s. The oldest university that still exists today is probably the University of Nanjing, in China. It was founded in 258 BC – over 2,250 years ago.

Grammar 4B
was / were

Complete the conversation with *was / were* (✔) or *wasn't / weren't* (✗).

A: Hi. Are you OK?

B: I phoned Sonia last night. She (1) _____ (✗) very happy. Her final exam results (2) _____ (✗) very good. The exams (3) _____ (✔) really difficult, she said. I don't understand it. She (4) _____ (✔) always a good student at school.

A: You (5) _____ (✔) the same, remember. You (6) _____ (✗) a good student at university.

B: That's true. I (7) _____ (✗) a good student. I (8) _____ (✔) more interested in other things, like the theatre.

A: Perhaps Sonia has other interests too!

Grammar 5A
Questions with was / were

Complete the questions and answers with the correct option.

A: When (1) *was / were* you born?

B: I was born in 1930, in Liverpool in England.

A: So when (2) *was / were* you at school?

B: I was at secondary school in the 1940s.

A: Where (3) *was / were* your school?

B: It was very near my house.

A: (4) *Was / Were* it very big?

B: No, it (5) *wasn't / weren't*.

A: What (6) *was / were* your teachers like?

B: They weren't very friendly. They were quite scary.

A: (7) *Was / Were* there a lot of students in the class.

B: Yes, there (8) *was / were*. There were about 40 students.

A: And how long (9) *was / were* you at school?

B: I was at school until I was fifteen. Then I started work.

Grammar 5B
Questions with was / were

Complete the interview with the correct form of *was* and *were* and a subject if necessary.

B: Let's play the famous person game! I think of an important person. You ask questions to identify him or her. I can tell you that she was a woman.

B: (1) _____ an actor?

A: No, she (2) _____. She was a writer, philosopher and teacher.

B: Where (3) _____ from?

A: She was from Russia originally, but she became a US citizen in 1931.

B: (4) _____ her books popular?

A: Yes, they (5) _____. Her books were very popular. She also wrote film scripts.

B: She was a philosopher too. What (6) _____ called?

A: Her ideas were called Objectivism.

B: And where (7) _____ a teacher?

A: She was a teacher at a number of American universities.

B: I don't recognise her. What (8) _____?

A: Her name was Ayn Rand.

Work & Study

Vocabulary 1A
Jobs

Match the jobs in the box to the pictures.

architect	doctor	engineer	scientist	lawyer
teacher				

1 _____   2 _____

3 _____   4 _____

5 _____   6 _____

Vocabulary 1B
Jobs

Complete the jobs.

Job	Description
1 d_____	Works in a hospital
2 o_____	Works in an office
3 s_____	Works in a laboratory
4 a_____	Designs houses and other buildings
5 e_____	Designs engines, motors and other machines
6 s_____	Helps people to play a sport
7 t_____	Works in a school or university
8 l_____	Helps people with legal problems

Vocabulary 2
Abilities

Complete the puzzle.

Across

2 You do this with a pencil. (4)

3 You do this in a swimming pool. (4)

4 You do this in a disco or nightclub. (4)

Down

1 Children do this in a park. (4)

2 You do this in a car. (5)

3 Some people do this in the shower! (4)

Vocabulary 3A
Types of school

Complete the table with the schools in the box. There are two schools you don't need to use.

college	high school	boarding school	kindergarten
primary school	medical college	elementary school	
law school	technical college	secondary school	

Situation	School
1 I want to be a lawyer.	
2 I live in the US. My children are 2 and 4 years old.	
3 My son wants to be a doctor.	
4 I live in the UK. My daughter's 15.	
5 I'm 17. I want to be a car mechanic.	
6 My sister's 19. She wants to study mathematics in the US.	
7 We live in the UK. We need a school for our children when we go to work in Kenya for 6 months.	
8 We live in New York. Our boy's 10.	

Work & Study

Vocabulary 3B
Types of school

Complete the welcome note with types of school.

Hi! Welcome to the UK! My name's Sarah, and I live at number 53. I have three children. Mark's 19 and he studies science at (1) _____ . Linda's 14 and she goes to secondary school – that's (2) _____ school in the US. And Jamie's 9 and goes to (3) _____ school – elementary school, you say. I know you have very young children. They can go to the local (4) _____ school (kindergarten). It's really good.

My husband and I are both teachers. I train people to be lawyers at the (5) _____ school, and Frank gives art and photography classes at the (6) _____ college. There are a lot of schools in this area! There's also an excellent (7) _____, with a good selection of books and films on DVD.

Vocabulary 4A
School subjects

Match the school subjects in the box to the pictures.

| chemistry | geography | ICT | history | maths | PE |

1 _____

2 _____

3 _____

4 _____

5 _____

6 _____

Vocabulary 4B
School subjects

Look at the exam questions and write the name of the school subject.

1   How many legs do spiders have?
    Subject: b_____

2   Who was the first emperor of China?
    Subject: h_____

3   What's the capital city of Nigeria?
    Subject: g_____

4   How do you say 'hello' in Spanish, Hindi and Chinese?
    Subject: l_____

5   What liquid is made of hydrogen and oxygen?
    Subject: c_____

6   What does c represent in $e=mc^2$?
    Subject: p_____

Extend your vocabulary
a (little) bit

Put the words in the correct order to make sentences.

1   was / school / a bit / Peter / at / lazy /.

    _____

2   home town / rough / a little bit / is / My /.

    _____

3   *The Sixth Sense* / is / scary / a little bit / The film /.

    _____

4   a bit / like / difficult / I / it's / but / maths /.

    _____

5   but / expensive / great / mobile's / it's / This / a bit /.

    _____

6   I wasn't good at geography. was / boring / a little bit / It /.

    _____

Work & Study

Pronunciation 1
Can

🔵 **1.18** Listen and choose the correct pronunciation of *can* and *can't*. Circle your answers.

1 I can't understand this. It's in Japanese.
   a /kənt/
   b /kɑːnt/

2 Can you read Japanese?
   a /kən/
   b /kæn/

3 No, I can't.
   a /kənt/
   b /kɑːnt/

4 But Jorgen can speak Japanese.
   a /kən/
   b /kæn/

5 Can you give me his number?
   a /kən/
   b /kæn/

6 Yes, I can. It's in my diary.
   a /kən/
   b /kæn/

Pronunciation 2
Two-syllable words

🔵 **1.19** Listen to the words. Is the stress on the first or second syllable? Tick (✔) your answers.

		First	Second
1	physics		
2	language		
3	teacher		
4	pencil		
5	English		
6	hotel		
7	doctor		
8	lawyer		
9	thriller		
10	cartoon		
11	August		
12	July		

Listening
Learning at home

🔵 **1.20** Listen to an interview about learning at home and complete the sentences with the correct option.

1 Children learn with *a parent / a teacher / a parent or teacher*.

2 Children who learn at home generally do *well / badly* in tests.

3 Some parents think schools are *difficult / unfriendly / very traditional*.

4 Some parents choose home schooling when there isn't a school *in their country / near their house*.

5 Home schooling is an option *in the US only / the US and the UK only / a lot of different countries*.

6 Karl thinks it's important for children who study at home to *meet other children / play sports / make friends at the local school*.

Work & Study

Reading
Person of the Century

1 Try to complete the fact file about Albert Einstein.

Born: In 1879 in (1) _____.

Profession: Scientist and university (2) _____.

Nobel Prize: In (3) _____ (1921).

Instrument: He played the (4) _____.

2 Read the profile of Einstein. Check or complete the fact file in exercise 1.

3 Complete the sentences with the correct options. Then read the profile again to check your answers.

1 He *was / wasn't* a very good student at school.
2 He *was / wasn't* quick to learn to speak when he was a child.
3 He *was / wasn't* a teacher in a school.
4 He *was / wasn't* always interested in maths and science.
5 A lot of scientists *can / can't* understand his ideas.
6 He *was / wasn't* famous during his life.
7 He *was / wasn't* good at answering letters.
8 We *have / don't have* one explanation for all the basic ideas in physics today.

4 Find these words in the profile. Use them to complete the sentences below.

later	from	first	then	before	after

1 Einstein was born in Germany. _____. He lived in Switzerland.
2 Einstein changed his nationality a number of times. _____ he was German. _____ he was Swiss. When he died he was American.
3 _____ 1933 to 1955, Einstein lived in the US.
4 Einstein was a Nobel prize winner _____ he moved to the US, and he became a celebrity _____ he moved to America.

5 Complete the profile of Wolfgang Mozart with the adverb form of the adjectives in brackets.

Mozart was born in Salzburg in 1756, and he is (1) _____ (*possible*) the greatest musical prodigy of all time. He learned to play the piano and violin very (2) _____ (*quick*) and he composed music very (3) _____ (*good*) from an early age. As a child, he travelled (4) _____ (*constant*) around Europe, and perhaps as a result, he was never a healthy person and he died young. His music has an individual style, and we can recognise it (5) _____ (*immediate*) today.

A profile of Albert Einstein

Albert Einstein and Mozart are possibly the two most famous examples of a genius. But unlike Mozart, Einstein wasn't a prodigy. Born in Germany in 1879, he was slow to learn to speak, and he was a normal student at school. He was interested in maths and science, but he preferred to study at home. Later, he studied to be a teacher, but he didn't find a job in a school and for some years was an office worker. A lot of Einstein's most famous ideas were the result of study in his free time, when he also played the violin to relax.

From 1908, he was a university teacher for many years, first in Europe and then in the US. He was the winner of the Nobel Prize in Physics in 1921. He is famous for his theories of relativity, but only a small number of scientists can understand them. His ambition was to find one explanation for the basic ideas in physics, but he died before this was possible.

Einstein was also a celebrity and he received letters from people around the world. Some of the letters were from children and he always answered them. One letter was from a girl with maths problems at school. 'Do not worry about your difficulties in Mathematics' was his answer. 'I can assure you my problems are still greater.'

Einstein was *Time* magazine's Person of the Century. But a century after his most important scientific ideas, we still don't have one explanation for the basic ideas in physics.

Glossary

ambition (*noun*) – a thing you want to do

genius (*noun*) – an extremely intelligent or talented person

prodigy (*noun*) – a prodigy learns to do a difficult activity when they are very young

theory (*noun*) – a collection of ideas that explains something

Work & Study

Writing
Applying for a training course

Reading

1 Read the list of training courses and the job application email. What course does the writer want to do?

Adult Training Centre

Training courses online or at our centre in Dublin, Ireland. Official qualifications.

Information Technology
Fashion design
Typing
Teaching English as a foreign language

Apply with a CV and letter to Irial O'Roirdan.
Email: applications@ATC.com

Dear Mr O'Roirdan,

I saw your advertisement for adult training courses on the internet and I would like to apply for a course in _____. The online option is best for me because I live in Hong Kong.

I am interested in the course because I would like to change my job and travel to other countries, and I need an official qualification. I work in an office at the moment.

I attach a copy of my CV. As you can see, I studied English at university, so I speak English very well. I was also an assistant teacher in an English school for a year. I'm good at using the internet and have a lot of experience of online learning.

If necessary, I am available for a telephone interview at any time.

I look forward to hearing from you.

Yours sincerely,

Ray Chén Yam-kuen

---

2 Read the email again and complete the interviewer's notes.

Name: (1) _____
From: (2) _____
Reasons for choosing course: He wants to
(3) _____ and needs (4) _____
Current job / studies: (5) _____
Education: (6) _____
Level of English: (7) _____
Previous experience: He was
(8) _____ for a year.

Writing skills: because and so

3 Look at the explanation. Then choose *because* or *so* in the sentences.

because + reason / explanation
so + consequence / result

1 I studied ICT at school *so / because* I'm good with computers.
2 I want to study to be a sports coach *so / because* I like working with people.
3 I cannot come for an interview next week *so / because* I will be on holiday.
4 I live near Dublin *so / because* I can study at the centre.
5 I was good at maths at school *so / because* I think accounting is a good job for me.

Language focus: prepositions

4 Complete the sentences with the correct preposition. Then look at the email to check your answers.

1 I saw your advertisement _____ the internet.
2 I'd like to apply _____ a course _____ accounting.
3 I am interested _____ the course because …
4 I studied geography _____ university.
5 I'm good _____ typing.
6 I have some experience _____ training sports people.
7 I am available _____ an interview any day next week.

Work & Study

Preparing to write

5 Choose a course from exercise 1 or another course you would like to do and make notes for a job application. Divide your notes into the paragraphs below.

Paragraph 1:

Where you saw the advertisement

What course you want to apply for

Paragraph 2:

Why you are interested in the course

Your job or studies

Paragraph 3:

Mention the information in your CV – education, jobs, skills, experience, etc.

Paragraph 4:

When you can have an interview

Writing

Write your job application email. Use your notes and the Useful phrases to help you. Remember to start and finish your email correctly.

Useful phrases

- *I saw your advertisement on the internet / in a newspaper.*
- *I work in an office / for a big company / at a university.*
- *I attach a copy of my CV.*
- *As you can see, I studied English at university / was good at maths at school / have a degree in history.*
- *If necessary, I am available for an interview at any time / any day this week / any afternoon.*

Grammar 1A
Past simple (regular verbs)

Complete the article with the past simple form of the verbs in brackets.

> **The history of free newspapers**
>
> The history of free daily newspaper
> (1) _____ (start) in the 1940s. A publisher
> from California (2) _____ (decide) to
> publish a free newspaper, the *Contra Costa Times*.
> The newspaper (3) _____ (use) advertising
> to pay for its production.
>
> In the 1970s, students from the University of
> Colorado in the USA (4) _____ (produce)
> a free daily newspaper called the *Colorado Daily*.
> When it began, it was only for students, but later it
> (5) _____ (carry) news about the lives of
> the local people.
>
> In 1995, *Metro* (6) _____ (publish) a free
> daily newspaper in Sweden. *Metro* then started to
> produce free newspapers in other countries, first in
> Europe, and then around the world.
>
> In 2005, a company in London (7) _____
> (create) the first free daily newspaper for business
> news, called *City A.M.*

Grammar 1B
Past simple (regular verbs)

Complete the second sentence with the past simple of the underlined verb in the first sentence.

1 Today, men and women <u>present</u> the news. When my grandparents were young, only men _____ the news.
2 I <u>listen</u> to radio stations on my computer. My grandparents _____ to the radio.
3 I <u>use</u> a computer to write important letters. They _____ a typewriter.
4 I <u>watch</u> a colour digital TV. They _____ a black and white TV.
5 I <u>study</u> online. My grandparents _____ in class with a teacher.

6 A lot of people <u>stop</u> studying when they're twenty or more. They _____ studying when they were sixteen.

Grammar 2
Past time expressions

It's Wednesday at 8pm. Match sentences 1–6 with the time expressions a–f.

1 I watched a film on Sunday night. _____
2 The President of Brazil visited my country last Friday. _____
3 We watched the news at 6pm. _____
4 I used the internet to book a hotel last night. _____
5 My local football team played in the cup final on Saturday. _____
6 Our son started a new job yesterday morning. _____

a four days ago
b two hours ago
c thirty-six hours ago
d three days ago
e twenty-four hours ago
f five days ago

Grammar 3A
Past simple (irregular verbs)

Put the verbs in the correct position in the table.

went	ask	hear	got	heard	have	spy
phone	leave	stop	write	saw	had	wrote
asked	walked	made	walk	spied	get	make
phoned	left	see	stopped	go		

Regular verbs		Irregular verbs	
Infinitive	Past simple	Infinitive	Past simple
answer	answered		
		see	saw
		write	wrote

News & Weather

Grammar 3B
Past simple (irregular verbs)

Complete the article with the past simple form of the verbs in brackets.

> **True stories**
>
> Erin Brockovich is from Kansas in the US. People first (1) _____ (hear) her story when Universal (2) _____ (make) a film about it.
>
> In the early 1990s, Erin (3) _____ (go) to live in California and she (4) _____ (get) a job as an office worker with a company of lawyers and one day she (5) _____ (see) some medical records. A lot of people from a town in California (6) _____ (have) similar health problems. She (7) _____ (know) something was wrong, and discovered that pollution by a big company caused the problems.
>
> Erin Brockovich (8) _____ (become) a TV presenter and today she travels round the world to tell other people her story.

Grammar 4
it

Write B's answers again with *it*.

A: Hi, Miranda. What time is it?
B: The time's 6 am.
 (1) _____.
A: I'm sorry! I forgot about the time difference. What's the weather like?
B: The weather's sunny. But the temperature's cold.
 (2) _____. But (3) _____.
A: And what about the hotel?
B: The hotel's great. I like the hotel.
 (4) _____. (5) _____.
A: Is the food good?
B: No, the food isn't.
 (6) _____.
A: Is the room comfortable?
B: Yes, the room is. The room has good views.
 (7) _____.(8) _____.

Grammar 5A
Past simple (questions and negative)

Put the words in the correct order to make questions.

A: (1) you / did / Where / go / ?
_____
B: We went to the beach.
A: (2) did / How / travel / you / ?
_____
B: We went by car.
A: (3) with / Who / you / go / did / ?
_____
B: We went with some friends.
A: (4) have / you / Did / good / time / a / ?
_____
B: Yes, we did.
A: (5) What / did / there / you / do / ?
_____
B: We played beach volleyball.
A: (6) swim / in / you / Did / the / sea / ?
_____
B: No, we didn't. The water was really cold.

Grammar 5B
Past simple (questions and negative)

Complete the questions and short answers with the correct form of the past simple and the subject in brackets.

A: Where (1) _____ (you / go) on holiday?
B: I went to DisneySea in Tokyo with my wife and son.
A: (2) _____ (you / drive) there?
B: No, we didn't. We went by train.
A: (3) _____ (you / have) a good time?
B: Yes, we (4) _____ but the weather wasn't very good.
A: (5) _____ (your son / visit) all the sights with you?
B: No, he (6) _____, he's still a little young for some of them.
A: What (7) _____ (you / like) best?
B: The Tower of Terror.
A: How (8) _____ (it / feel)?
B: It was really exciting!

News & Weather

Grammar 6
Past simple (negative)

Complete the first sentence with the negative form of the verb in the second sentence.

1 We ＿＿＿＿＿＿ to India. We went to Sri Lanka.
2 I ＿＿＿＿＿＿ a bad time. I had a good time.
3 Renuka ＿＿＿＿＿＿ friends. She visited family.
4 We ＿＿＿＿＿＿ Renuka's uncle. We saw her cousins.
5 I ＿＿＿＿＿＿ Dilipa. I knew Amanthi.
6 We ＿＿＿＿＿＿ with her family. We stayed in a hotel.
7 I ＿＿＿＿＿＿ any postcards. I wrote emails.
8 We ＿＿＿＿＿＿ back yesterday. We got back three days ago.

Vocabulary 1
Prepositions of time and place

Complete the biography with the prepositions *at*, *in*, *on* and *to*.

Biography: Angela Rippon

Angela Rippon is a British television journalist. She was born (1) ＿＿＿＿＿＿ the 12 October 1944 (2) ＿＿＿＿＿＿ Devon (3) ＿＿＿＿＿＿ England. She studied (4) ＿＿＿＿＿＿ a grammar school in Plymouth, and then worked for a newspaper. Her work in television started (5) ＿＿＿＿＿＿ the BBC (British Broadcasting Corporation) in Plymouth. Then, (6) ＿＿＿＿＿＿ 1974, she started reading the news on the national channel BBC2 and was the world's first woman to be a permanent newsreader on television. She was one of the most famous people (7) ＿＿＿＿＿＿ the UK (8) ＿＿＿＿＿＿ the 1970s. In 1984 she moved (9) ＿＿＿＿＿＿ Boston (10) ＿＿＿＿＿＿ Massachusetts (11) ＿＿＿＿＿＿ the US, and worked for Channel 7, but she returned (12) ＿＿＿＿＿＿ the UK again after a short time and continued her television work there.

Extend your vocabulary
history and *story*

Complete the conversation with *story* or *history*.

A: There's an interesting (1) ＿＿＿＿＿＿ in the newspaper about a (2) ＿＿＿＿＿＿ teacher in France. Last Friday she started classes with her students about the (3) ＿＿＿＿＿＿ of ancient Rome. At the weekend, she discovered some Roman money in her garden.

B: Is that really true, or is it just a (4) ＿＿＿＿＿＿

A: It's true. She's a writer, too, and she wants to write a children's (5) ＿＿＿＿＿＿ about the Roman money.

Vocabulary 2A
Weather

Match the weather words with the pictures.

| clouds | freezing | rain | sun | wind |

1 ＿＿＿＿＿＿

2 ＿＿＿＿＿＿

3 ＿＿＿＿＿＿

4 ＿＿＿＿＿＿

5 ＿＿＿＿＿＿

News & Weather

Vocabulary 2B
Weather

Complete the description with weather and temperature words.

Wellington weather

The weather in Wellington in New Zealand is temperate. That means there are never extreme temperatures. It's (1) c_____ in July and August, but never (2) f_____ and it's (3) w_____ in January and February. It isn't often hot, and it's never (4) b_____. But the sun is very strong on (5) s_____ days. We get some rain every month, but the (6) r_____ months are May to August. It's never (7) s_____ – you need to go to the mountains to see snow. But it's often (8) w_____ That's because the wind is strong between New Zealand's two islands.

Pronunciation 1
The past simple

1.21 Listen to the sentences. Is -ed an extra syllable or not? Tick (✔) your answers.

		-ed **is an extra syllable:** /ɪd/	-ed **isn't an extra syllable**
1	I visited Hanoi.		
2	I stayed at a hotel.		
3	I wanted to see an old friend.		
4	I looked for his number.		
5	I picked up the phone.		
6	I phoned his number.		
7	I waited.		
8	The answer phone started.		
9	I listened to the message.		
10	The message ended.		
11	I decided to leave a message.		
12	He called me the next day.		

Pronunciation 2
/w/ and /h/

1.22 Listen to the sentences. Choose the number of /w/ or /h/ sounds in each sentence.

/w/

1 Who did William see on Wednesday?
   1 / 2 / 3

2 Where does Wendy work?
   1 / 2 / 3

3 When was the weather windy?
   3 / 4 / 5

4 When was William in Winchester?
   2 / 3 / 4

/h/

5 How many hours do you have to help me?
   2 / 3 / 4

6 Who did Henry have lunch with?
   2 / 3 / 4

Listening
Where do you get your news?

1.23 Read the sentences below. Then listen to three interviews in the street. Which speaker does these things – 1, 2 or 3?

1 Speaker _____ thinks the news is always bad.
2 Speaker _____ reads newspapers online.
3 Speaker _____ reads free newspapers.
4 Speaker _____ watches the news on TV.
5 Speaker _____ only watches sports news.
6 Speaker _____ read a newspaper this morning.
7 Speaker _____ sometimes listens to the radio.
8 Speaker _____ gets news from the radio.
9 Speaker _____ doesn't follow the news

News & Weather

Reading
Clouds

1 Quickly read the article from an online encyclopaedia. Which three words or phrases are names for clouds? Circle your answers.

stratus   water vapour   Luke Howard   cirrus   Latin
storm   cumulonimbus

What are clouds?

Clouds are usually made of drops of water and sometimes ice crystals. They start as an invisible gas called 'water vapour', and the water vapour produces clouds when the temperature of the air is at the 'dew point'. At this temperature, the water vapour becomes liquid water. This water collects on dust particles in the air, and makes the clouds we see. If clouds form on the ground, we call them fog.

Where do their names come from?

Before 1800, clouds didn't have names, and people didn't understand them very well. The names we use were the idea of an English chemist called Luke Howard. He studied clouds in his free time, and he suggested Latin names for them in a scientific paper in 1802.

What types of cloud are there?

Howard classified clouds into three basic types. The first is called *cumulus* – big, tall clouds with a clear shape. The second type is called *stratus* – long, flat clouds. These are the flat clouds that make the sky grey on a cloudy day. The third type is called *cirrus* – thin, soft clouds, like hair, and the highest clouds in the sky.

He then used combinations of these names to describe clouds in more detail, and used the Latin word *nimbus* (meaning *rain*) to describe a rain cloud. A common example is the *cumulonimbus* cloud – the cloud of storms. Meteorologists started using Howard's cloud names, and continue to use them today.

Glossary

drop (*noun*) – a very small piece of water. You see water drops when it rains

dust particle (*noun*) – a small piece of dust. Dust collects on things in your house when you don't clean it

ice crystal (*noun*) – a very small piece of ice. Water becomes ice at 0°C

invisible (*adjective*) – if something is invisible, you can't see it

News & Weather

2 Read the first two sections of the article again and answer the questions.

1 What are clouds made of?

_____

2 What is water vapour?

_____

3 What happens at the 'dew point'?

_____

4 Before we can see clouds, what does water do?

_____

5 What's the name for clouds on the ground?

_____

6 What did Luke Howard suggest?

_____

3 Read the third section of the article and write the name of the clouds under the pictures.

1 _____

2 _____

3 _____

4 Test you memory. Complete the sentences with the past simple positive or negative of the verbs in brackets. Then look at the article again to check your answers.

1 Clouds _____ (have) names in 1800.

2 People _____ (understand) clouds very well in 1800.

3 Luke Howard _____ (write) a scientific paper in 1802.

4 He _____ (be) a meteorologist.

5 He _____ (use) combinations of four Latin names to describe clouds.

6 Meteorologists _____ (start) using his names for clouds.

News & Weather

Writing
Describing a weather experience

Reading

1 Read the description from an internet news site and put the weather in the correct order.

a It started to rain heavily and there was a strong wind.

b It was sunny.

c There was a huge storm.

d It was extremely hot and sunny.

1 _____   2 _____   3 _____   4 _____

○○○

Write and tell us about your weather experiences!

This happened two years ago when we were at a folk festival in the French Pyrenees. The festival lasts for six days and it takes place every year, one year in France, and the next year in Spain.

When we arrived the weather was fantastic. It was extremely hot and sunny, so we went to the campsite and put up our tent. But in the mountains the weather can change quickly. That night there was a huge storm. At first we weren't worried, but it started to rain heavily and there was a strong wind. A little later, water started coming into the tent. In the end, we decided to take our things and go to a hotel. There weren't any rooms free but they let us sleep on the floor in the dining room. The next morning it was sunny again. But our tent wasn't there. The wind blew it away during the night.

David, Boston

2 Read the description again and complete the sentences.

1 The festival lasts

_____.

2 The festival takes place

_____.

3 When they arrived the weather was

_____.

4 The first night there was

_____.

5 They slept

_____.

6 When they returned to the camp site,
   the tent _____ because

_____.

Language focus: adjectives & adverbs describing weather

3 What do the adjectives and adverbs describe? Read the description again to check your answers.

1 fantastic   _____

2 extremely   _____

3 huge   _____

4 heavily   _____

5 strong   _____

4 The adjectives below can all describe the weather. Tick (✔) the positive adjectives.

_____ awful   _____ beautiful   _____ great

_____ horrible   _____ terrible   _____ wonderful

Writing skills: time expressions

5 Find six more time expressions in the second paragraph of the description. Add them to the list below.

two years ago

_____

_____

_____

_____

_____

Preparing to write

6 Make notes about a time when you experienced extreme weather conditions. Answer the questions below and use adjectives, adverbs and time expressions.

When did it happen?

Where were you?

What was the weather like at first?

What happened next?

What happened in the end?

Writing

Write a description of a weather experience. Where were you? What happened? Use your notes and the Useful phrases to help you.

Useful phrases

- *This happened two years ago / last year / in 2009.*
- *We were at a festival / on holiday / at the beach / in the mountains.*
- *When we arrived / started our journey / left home …*
- *The weather can change very quickly.*
- *We decided to go to the hotel.*

Grammar 1A
Present continuous

Complete the conversations with the *-ing* form of the verbs.

A: What are you (1) _____ (do)?

B: I'm (2) _____ (phone) a taxi. It's late and I don't want to walk home.

A: Hi Lian. I'm (3) _____ (sit) on the bus. Where are you?

B: My father's (4) _____ (drive) me to university today.

A: You aren't (5) _____ (swim).

B: No. It's really cold. I'm (6) _____ (wait) for the sun to come out.

A: There's a lot of pollution today.

B: That's because the metro isn't (7) _____ (work), and more people are (8) _____ (use) their cars.

Grammar 1B
Present continuous

Complete the conversation with the present continuous form of the verbs in brackets.

A: Hi, Max! Where (1) _____ (you / go)?

B: Oh, hi, Mia. Hi, Leo. (2) I _____ (go) to work.

A: You (3) _____ (walk) very fast. Are you late?

B: Yes, I am. I normally go to work by car, but my wife (4) _____ (use) the car today.

A: (5) _____ (your children / walk) to school, too?

B: No, they aren't. Gina (6) _____ (take) them in the car.

A: Well, we (7) _____ (not work) today. We're on holiday. It (8) _____ (not rain) at the moment, so we (9) _____ (go) to the beach.

B: Lucky you!

Grammar 2
Present simple & present continuous

Complete the sentences with the correct option – the present simple or present continuous.

1 A: What *are you doing / do you do*?
   B: I'm an engineer. What's your job?

2 A: What *are you doing / do you do*?
   B: I want to turn up the TV, but I can't. It's really quiet.

3 *I'm travelling / I travel* to Istanbul a lot at the moment. We have a new contract with a Turkish company.

4 A: *Does the 55 go / Is the 55 going* to the city centre?
   B: No. You need to take the 43.

5 *I read / I'm reading* a really interesting book at the moment. It's about the history of the motorbike.

6 Hiro *studies / 's studying* maths at university. It's his final year, so he *studies / 's studying* a lot for his final exams this month.

Grammar 3A
The comparative

Complete the opinions with the comparative form of the adjectives in brackets.

'I prefer beach holidays. They're (1) _____ (cheap) and my children are (2) _____ (happy) because they can play in the sea. Cities are (3) _____ (noisy) and (4) _____ (hot) than beach destinations.'

'I think city holidays are (5) _____ (good). Cities are (6) _____ (busy) than beach destinations. They're (7) _____ (interesting), and there's a (8) _____ (large) selection of things to do.'

Grammar 3B
The comparative

Complete the sentences using the words and the comparative form of the adjective. Don't forget *than!*

1 Brazil / warm / Canada.
   Brazil's _____.

2 Holidays / nice / work.
   Holidays are _____.

3 Greece / sunny / Scotland.
   Greece is _____.

Coming & Going

4 Trains / big / buses.

Trains are _____.

5 Cars / expensive / bikes.

Cars are _____.

6 Winter weather / bad / summer weather.

Winter weather is _____.

Grammar 4A
The infinitive of purpose

Match the questions 1–6 with the answers a–f.

Why do people …

1 emigrate? _____

2 go on holiday? _____

3 study languages? _____

4 walk to work? _____

5 use cars? _____

6 watch the news? _____

a To relax and see different places.

b To do some exercise.

c To have a better life.

d To know what's happening in the world.

e To communicate with other people.

f To travel quickly to other places.

Grammar 4B
The infinitive of purpose

Complete the text with the infinitives in the box.

to teach   to have   to see   to communicate   to help

I joined the organisation VSO (1) _____
people in countries with economic problems. First, the
organization interviewed me (2) _____ what
skills and abilities I had. Then they sent me to Beni, in
Nepal, (3) _____ English in a school. People
here need English (4) _____ with tourists and
(5) _____ better work opportunities in the
future.

Vocabulary 1A
Transport

Match the transport words in the box with the pictures.

| bicycle / bike   boat   on foot   metro   train
motorcycle / motorbike |
|---|

1 _____   2 _____

3 _____   4 _____

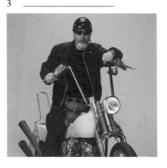

5 _____   6 _____

Vocabulary 1B
Transport

Complete the descriptions with transport words.

How do you get to work?

'I live in Barcelona, Spain. There's a service here called
Bicing. I can hire a (1) _____ and cycling is
good exercise. On rainy days, I take the
(2) _____. It's under the ground, but it's fast.'

'I usually go on (3) _____ and can walk to work
in 25 minutes. When I'm late, I go on my
(4) _____. It's a small one, but it's fast in traffic.

'I live in Venice, Italy. There's lots of water in the city, so I
go to work by (5) _____.'

'I'm a commuter so I always take the (6) _____
to work. I can sit with my computer and work for an hour.'

Coming & Going

Vocabulary 2A
Big numbers

Match numbers 1–8 with words a–h.

1 200   _____
2 255   _____
3 2,000   _____
4 2,055   _____
5 2,500   _____
6 2,555   _____
7 25,000   _____
8 25,500   _____

a two thousand
b twenty-five thousand
c two thousand five hundred
d twenty-five thousand five hundred
e two hundred
f two thousand and fifty-five
g two thousand five hundred and fifty-five
h two hundred and fifty-five

Vocabulary 2B
Big numbers

Write the big numbers as words.

1 1,000 = a _____
2 3,600 = three _____ six _____
3 68,000 = _____-eight _____
4 479,000 = four _____ and seventy-nine _____
5 48,391 = _____-eight _____ three _____ and _____-one
6 2,750 = two _____

Extend your vocabulary
come and go

Complete the conversation with the correct verbs.

A: Hello, Marin speaking.
B: Hi. It's Fred. Can you (1) *come / go* to my office for a moment?
A: OK. I'm just (2) *coming / going*.
A: Hi. What is it?
B: You know Judy's leaving and (3) *coming / going* to live in Thailand.
A: Yes.

B: Well, I'm organising a surprise party on Saturday at 8. Can you (4) *come / go*?
A: I can't. I'm (5) *coming / going* to a concert. But I can (6) *come / go* for the first hour. The concert starts at 10.00.
B: Great. You can (7) *come / go* back to your office now.
A: Sorry?
B: Judy's (8) *coming / going* back from lunch now. I don't want her to see us talking.
A: Oh, OK.

Vocabulary 3A
Feelings about travel

Complete the messages with the adjectives in the box.

| angry | bored | happy | nervous | sad | worried |

1 We're finally going on holiday! It's fantastic! I'm really _____!
2 We're at the airport. Sebastian's really _____. He hates planes.
3 There's a problem with the flight. We can't leave. The kids are really hungry, but there isn't any food. I'm getting really _____!
4 We're still at the airport. There aren't any activities for children. We don't have any books or toys. They're getting _____.
5 Now I can't find my passport. Did I leave it at home? I'm really _____. If I can't find it, I can't fly.
6 First the good news. We're here! The bad news is the place isn't very nice. It's noisy and there are just hotels. And it's cloudy. I'm a bit _____.

Vocabulary 3B
Feelings about travel

Complete the adjectives.

Often, people feel …
1 h_____ on holiday.
2 s_____ when their holiday finishes.
3 w_____ when they have money problems.
4 n_____ before a difficult journey.
5 b_____ on long flights.
6 a_____ when their train arrives late.
But this isn't always true!

Coming & Going

Vocabulary 4
Things to take abroad

Complete the list of things to take with you.

1 c_____

2 c_____

3 p_____

4 w_____

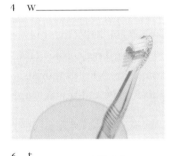

5 s_____

6 t_____

Pronunciation 1
The /ŋ/ sound

🔘 **1.24** Underline the words with the /ŋ/ sound. Then listen and check your answers.

1 England's in the United Kingdom.
2 They're having a meeting in Singapore.
3 I think there's something in the fridge.
4 We're watching a boring film.
5 This evening we want to sing in a karaoke bar.
6 He's travelling to China by train.

Pronunciation 2
Weak and strong forms

🔘 **1.25** Listen and circle the pronunciation of the underlined words.

		Strong form	Weak form
1	Is it true that the Reeds <u>have</u> moved?	/hæv/	/həv/
2	Yes, they <u>have</u>.	/hæv/	/həv/
3	Where did they go <u>to</u>?	/tuː/	/tə/
4	They went <u>to</u> Spain.	/tuː/	/tə/
5	I hope you <u>can</u> contact them.	/kæn/	/kən/
6	Yes, I <u>can</u>.	/kæn/	/kən/
7	Here's <u>the</u> address.	/ðiː/	/ðə/
8	And here's <u>the</u> phone number they left.	/ðiː/	/ðə/

Listening
Tips for long flights

🔘 **1.26** Read the tips for long flights and choose the correct options. Then listen to the radio programme and check your answers.

Useful tips for long flights

1 *Do / Don't* do exercises in your seat.
2 *Stand up / Don't stand up* and walk in the plane.
3 *Sit / Don't sit* next to an emergency exit.
4 *Drink / Don't drink* lots of water before your flight.
5 *Drink / Don't drink* coffee or tea.
6 *Change / Don't change* the time on your watch to the time at your destination.

Coming & Going

Reading
Railway records

1 Match the famous train journeys to the descriptions.

1   The Trans-Siberian Railway _____

2   The Orient Express _____

3   The Peruvian Central Railway _____

4   The Quinghai-Tibet Railway _____

a   This goes from Xining in central China to Lhasa in Tibet.

b   This goes from Paris in France to Istanbul in Turkey.

c   This goes from Moscow in the west of Russia to Vladivostok in the east.

d   This line crosses the Andes mountain range.

2 Look quickly at the travel report. Which train journey from exercise 1 is it about?

3 Read the report and complete the travel information.

City	Time	Distance (kilometres)
Xining	20:07	
Golmud	(1)	(3)
Lhasa	(2)	(4)

4 Read the report again and correct the sentences.

1   The weather in Xining is often good.

_____

2   It's longer than all other railways in the world.

_____

3   To feel good at Tanggula Pass, all passengers need oxygen.

_____

4   The second section of the track took 12 years to build.

_____

5   The writer has good views of the Himalayas when he arrives in Lhasa.

_____

6   He used oxygen on the journey.

_____

7   He has a negative opinion of the journey.

_____

5 Find and correct four grammar mistakes in this text.

The transport network in China grows. An example of this is the Qinghai-Tibet railway. This is going from Xining to Lhasa. The journey takes more long than a day to complete. A lot of tourists go to Lhasa for see the Potala palace, the traditional home of Tibet's Dalai Lamas.

Railway records

Xining: 20:00

I'm at the railway station in Xining, the capital city of the Chinese province of Qinghai. Qinghai is on the northeast part of the Tibetan Plateau, and Xining is about 2,200 metres above sea level. It's often cold, and often windy. I'm waiting for the N917 train to Llasa, in Tibet. The length of my journey is 1,956 kilometres, but this isn't what makes it special. Many other train journeys are longer, but no train line in the world is higher.

Golmud: 9:30

It's morning and we're now in Golmud, Qinghai's second city. The Chinese government completed the 815 kilometres section of track between Xining and Golmund in 1984. The next section began in 1984, but was much more difficult to build and didn't open until July 2006. Before it arrives in Lhasa it crosses the Tanggula Pass. At this point the train is at 5,072 metres above sea level, making it the highest railway in the world, and about 200 metres higher than the Peruvian railway in the Andes. At this altitude a lot of people feel bad and have headaches, so the train has extra oxygen for us to use, and you can lie down if you feel unwell.

Lhasa: 22:30

26 hours and 23 minutes after leaving Xining, we're finally in Lhasa, at 3,650 metres high. It's dark now and I can't see the snowy peaks of the Himalayas in the background, but the views during the journey were fantastic! I didn't need any oxygen but had a bit of a headache. But this is definitely one of the world's great railway experiences.

Coming & Going

Writing
Writing a report
Reading

1 Read the report about a city. Who is it for?

1 People who live in the city.

2 People visiting the city for a film festival.

3 People visiting the city for a day.

---

1 _____

It's easy to get to the city by train and by bus. International visitors can fly to the capital city and catch a train. The journey takes about 50 minutes. There are frequent buses from the airport, too, and these are cheaper. Another option is to hire a car, but it's difficult to park in the city.

2 _____

A good way to travel around the city is by bus or on foot. The centre's quite small, and the buses are very efficient. Traffic gets heavy when people are going to and from work, so walking is probably a better option at those times. Visitors can get a taxi after evening films. It's sometimes difficult to find one, but this situation is getting better.

3 _____

There are a number of hotels in the city, and they are building two new hotels at the moment. There isn't a five-star hotel, but there are a few near the airport. There are a lot of bed-and-breakfasts and guest houses, and there's a big youth hostel, too.

---

2 Write the correct titles for the sections in the report. Use the titles in the box.

| Places to stay   Getting to the city   Travelling in the city |

3 Answer the questions.

1 How long does the journey take from the airport by bus?

_____

2 What other ways can people travel to the city?

_____

3 What are good ways to travel in the city? Why?

_____

4 What problem is there with taxis?

_____

Places to stay

4 Match the places to stay in the third section of the report with the definitions below.

1 a private house where you get a room for the night and breakfast in the morning

_____

2 a cheap place where travellers, especially young people, can stay

_____

3 a building where you stay in a room and have meals

_____

4 a private house where you get a room for the night

_____

Adjective + infinitive

5 Complete the sentences from the report with an infinitive. Then look at the report to check your answers.

1 It's easy _____ to the city by train and by bus.

2 It's difficult _____ in the city.

3 It's sometimes hard _____ a taxi.

Expressing options

6 Match 1–5 and a–e to make sentences from the report.

1 There are _____

2 Another option is _____

3 A good way to travel _____

4 Walking is probably _____

5 Visitors can _____

a to hire a car.

b get a taxi.

c frequent buses from the airport.

d is by bus or on foot.

e a better option.

Preparing to write

7 Look at the titles from exercise 2. Make notes about your town/city, or one you have visited.

Coming & Going

Writing

Your town or city wants to organise one of these events:

- A festival
- A conference
- An international meeting

Write a report about the transport and accommodation options your town/city can offer for visitors to the event. Use your notes and the Useful phrases to help you.

Useful phrases

- *It's easy / difficult to get / find …*
- *The journey takes …*
- *Another / A better option is to hire / take …*
- *A good way to travel / see …*
- *Traffic gets heavy when …*
- *Visitors / You can get / find …*
- *There are a number of / (quite) a lot of / a few hotels …*

Life & Style

Grammar 1A
Present perfect

Complete each pair of sentences with the past participle of one of the verbs in the box.

| climb | visit | ride | swim | take | work |

1 I've _____ in the sea. I've never _____ in a lake.
2 We've _____ a camel. We haven't _____ a horse.
3 Has he ever _____ on a farm? Has he _____ at a zoo?
4 I've _____ Australia. I've never _____ New Zealand.
5 She's _____ photos of insects. She's never _____ any insects home.
6 Have you ever _____ a tree? Have you _____ a mountain?

Grammar 1B
Present perfect

Complete the interview with the present perfect form of the verbs in brackets or short answers.

A: (1) _____ (you / plan) your holidays?
B: Yes, we (2) _____. We're going on a safari in India. (3) _____ (you / ever / see) a tiger?
A: No, I (4) _____. Only in a zoo.
B: Well, that's what we want to do.
A: David (5) _____ (travel) to India before. (6) _____ (he / see) one?
B: No, he (7) _____. He (8) _____ (visit) cities, but he (8) _____ (not visit) any wildlife parks there.
A: Well, we (10) _____ (not decide) where to go. But I think I prefer a holiday by the sea!

Grammar 2A
The superlative

Complete the conversations with the superlative form of the adjectives in brackets.

1 A: What's the (1) _____ (good) age to have children?
  B: I had my (2) _____ (old) child when I was 25. That's a good age.
2 A: What's the (3) _____ (exciting) party you've been to?
  B: My brother's wedding party. It was also the (4) _____ (big). They invited 300 people!
3 A: Which of these wedding dresses is the (5) _____ (nice)?
  B: I like the white dress. It's the (6) _____ (traditional).
4 A: What's the (7) _____ (funny) festival you know about?
  B: La Tomatina festival in Spain. People throw tomatoes at you, so it's also the (8) _____ (dirty)!

Grammar 2B
The superlative

Are the underlined adjective forms in the sentences correct or incorrect? Circle your answers.

1 Some people think the Putignano Carnival in Italy is the <u>oldest</u> carnival in Europe.
  Correct / Incorrect
2 Inti Raymi is probably the <u>more</u> important festival in Peru.
  Correct / Incorrect
3 In Malaysia, people have their <u>biggest</u> birthday party when they're 21.
  Correct / Incorrect
4 Birthdays are <u>most exciting</u> for young people than for old people.
  Correct / Incorrect
5 Weddings are often <u>happiest</u> ceremony in a person's life.
  Correct / Incorrect
6 In many cultures, parents choose <u>the best</u> person for their child to marry.
  Correct / Incorrect

Life & Style

Grammar 3A
have got

Write the sentences again with *have got*.

1 I have two brothers.
_____ two brothers.

2 They have blue eyes and black hair.
_____ blue eyes and black hair.

3 Tom has lots of tattoos.
_____ lots of tattoos.

4 He doesn't have an ordinary job. He's a rock musician.
_____ an ordinary job. He's a rock musician.

5 Do you have any brothers or sisters?
_____ any brothers or sisters?

6 Does your brother have an unusual job?
_____ an unusual job?

Grammar 3B
have got

Complete the conversation with the correct forms of *have got*.

A: Have you met Inga?

B: I don't know.

A: She (1) _____ blonde hair and she's tall.

B: (2) _____ long hair?

A: No, she (3) _____. It's short. Her sister
(4) _____ exactly the same hairstyle.

B: (5) _____ a clothes shop in the market?

A: Yes, they (6) _____. Anyway, Inga needs to
learn German, but she (7) _____ a teacher.
Can you give her classes?

B: No, I (8) _____ time. But maybe Franz can.
(9) _____ his number?

A: No, I (10) _____.

B: Here it is.

Grammar 4
one & ones

Complete the conversation with *one* or *ones*.

A: I like that dress over there.

B: Which (1) _____?

A: The dark green (2) _____.

B: It's very formal. There are some nicer
(3) _____ over there.

A: You're right. They are nice.

B: I like those two.

A: Which (4) _____?

B: The red (5) _____ with long sleeves.

A: I prefer the white (6) _____.

B: Well, I need to get a jacket. This (7) _____ is
really old.

A: Why don't you look somewhere else? I saw a really
good (8) _____ in the shop opposite this
(9) _____.

B: OK, good idea.

Vocabulary 1A
Nature

Match the words to the pictures.

lake	insect	farm	river	bird	plant

1 _____   2 _____

3 _____   4 _____

5 _____   6 _____

Life & Style

Vocabulary 1B
Nature

Complete the puzzle.

Across

1 People play or go for a walk in a _____. (4)

3 Everest is the world's tallest _____. (8)

5 A _____ can fly. (4)

7 People produce food on a _____. (4)

9 The Caspian Sea is really a _____. (4)

10 The sequoia is the world's tallest _____.
   Some are 100 metres tall. (5)

Down

1 A _____ is normally green. We eat some
   types. (5)

2 People go to a _____ to see animals. (3)

4 Humans are a type of _____. (6)

6 A mosquito is a type of _____. (6)

7 _____ live in water. (4)

8 The Amazon in Brazil is the world's second longest
   _____. (5)

Vocabulary 2A
Life events

Complete the life events with the correct options.

1 He *was / got / had* born in 1940.

2 He *graduated / left / retired* school in 1956.

3 He *graduated / started / left* from university.

4 He *had / started / was* work when he was 21.

5 He *got / had / left* home when he was 23.

6 He *got / left / started* married two years later.

7 He *had / retired / started* a child.

8 He *graduated / left / retired* from work at the age of 60.

Vocabulary 2B
Life events

Complete the description with the correct words.

My aunt was (1) b_____ in 1940. Her family
didn't have much money, and she (2) l_____
school when she was 15 nd started (3) w_____.
She got (4) m_____ to my uncle when she was
18 and (5) h_____ the first of her three children
when she was 19. After that, she stayed at home with them
until they (6) l_____ home. When she was 40,
she decided to go to university. She (7) g_____
from university when she was 47 and worked as a teacher.
She retired (8) f_____ work when she was 60.

Life & Style

Vocabulary 3A
Parts of the body

Look at the picture. Match the parts of the body in the box to the numbers.

hand foot head leg shoulder arm

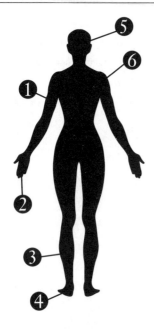

1 _____
2 _____
3 _____
4 _____
5 _____
6 _____

Vocabulary 3B
Parts of the body

Complete the descriptions with parts of the body. Use a plural if necessary.

Gorillas have a big (1) _____, long (2) _____ and short (3) _____.

Cows have four (4) _____ to digest their food. The best meat comes from a cow's (5) _____.

Human beings have a big (6) _____ compared to their body and their (7) _____ are made for running. They sometimes carry their children on their (8) _____.

Vocabulary 4
Parts of the face

Complete the sentences with parts of the face.

1 We use our m_____ to eat and speak.
2 We use our e_____ to listen and hear things.
3 We use our e_____ to look and see things.
4 We've got two c_____ on our face. Sometimes they go red.
5 We use our n_____ to smell food before we eat it.
6 We cut our h_____ because if not, it gets longer and longer.
7 We can recognise people because we've all got a different f_____.

Vocabulary 5A
Clothes

Match the clothes in the box with the pictures.

gloves jacket scarf shirt shorts skirt

1 _____   2 _____

3 _____   4 _____

5 _____   6 _____

Life & Style

Vocabulary 5B
Clothes

Circle the word that is different. Use the clues to help you.

1   socks   shorts   trousers   dress

Clue: You wear them on your feet.

2   gloves   jumper   scarf   T-shirt

Clue: You wear it in warm weather.

3   trousers   jeans   tie   shirt

Clue: They are informal.

4   hat   jacket   shirt   trousers

Clue: You wear them on your legs.

5   shoes   socks   trainers   shorts

Clue: You don't wear them on your feet.

6   jumper   T-shirt   hat   shirt

Clue: You wear it on your head.

Extend your vocabulary
Talking about colours

Look at the box and complete the sentences with light or dark.

1 He's wearing a _____ blue tie.

2 I hate _____ green T-shirts!

3 You always wear _____ blue clothes.

4 It was cold and the sky was _____ grey.

5 I like that _____ green sofa.

6 Look at those _____ grey clouds.

Pronunciation
/ʃ/ and /s/

🔊 **1.27** All the sentences have one /ʃ/ and one /s/ sound. Listen and underline the words with the /s/ sound.

1 You can't wear shorts with socks!

2 June normally wears a skirt and a shirt to work.

3 I see you have short hair now.

4 Have a shower before you swim.

5 My sisters are in a talent show.

6 I need to X-ray your stomach and your shoulder.

Listening
An interview about tourism

🔊 **1.28** Listen to a radio interview. Are the sentences about the traditional tourist industry (Trad), the ecotourist industry (Eco) or both types of industry (Trad & Eco)? Tick (✔) your answers.

	Trad	Eco	Trad & Eco
1 Destinations are usually cities and the beach.			
2 Destinations are natural places.			
3 Tourists want to see animal and plant species.			
4 Tourists change the places they visit.			
5 Tourists try to protect the local environment.			
6 Groups of tourists are big.			
7 Most money goes to the tourist company.			
8 Costa Rica is a very popular destination.			
9 It's getting bigger.			
10 Companies use 'ecotourist' in a false way.			

Life & Style

Reading
Body piercing

1 Do you think these sentences are true (*T*) or false (*F*)?

1 Body piercing is a very old custom.

2 Body piercing is only common in North America, Europe and Australasia.

3 The first piercings were in the nose.

4 Piercings have different meanings in different cultures.

5 Piercings were usually a female custom in the past.

2 Read the article and check your answers to exercise 1.

3 Read the article again and write the reasons for different piercings.

Coming of age   Getting married   Fashion
Status symbol

1 Reason: _____
_____

Examples: Men in North American cultures and in Shakespeare's time.

2 Reason: _____
_____

Examples: Boys in Borneo and men in Papua New Guinea.

3 Reason: _____
_____

Examples: Women in the Middle East and in Chad.

4 Reason: _____
_____

Examples: Young people today and men in Ancient Rome

4 What four other reasons for piercings does the article mention?

1 _____
_____

2 _____
_____

3 _____

4 _____
_____

5 Complete the interview with the correct form of the words in the box.

be   get married   good   have got   old   one

A: How many piercings have you got?

B: I (1) _____ about eighty in total.

A: Which are (2) _____ piercings you have?

B: The (3) _____ in my ears. I had them when I was a child.

A: You (4) _____ last year. Did you take out your rings and studs for the wedding?

B: No, I didn't. They're part of my appearance!

A: (5) _____ they ever _____ a problem at work?

B: No, they haven't. I work in a clothes shop, so my piercings are positive. That's (6) _____ thing about my job!

Life & Style

Piercing past and present

Today it's common to see young people in Western countries with piercings in different parts of the body. These piercings are usually a fashion. They are not acceptable in some formal situations, but they are not new. Piercings have been a custom or fashion in cultures around the world for thousands of years.

Ear piercings

These were the first type of piercing. The oldest example was on a 5,300-year-old body discovered under snow in the Alps between Austria and Italy. Julius Caesar introduced earrings as a fashion for men to Ancient Rome, and in William Shakespeare's time earrings were a status symbol – they showed you were rich and important. In Borneo today, boys have an ear piercing as part of a coming of age ceremony. The mother pierces one ear, and the father pierces the other one.

Nose piercings

Nose piercing started in the Middle East about 4,000 years ago, when men gave women a nose ring as a wedding gift. Today, Indian women wear a nose stud to help them have children. In other cultures, nose piercings have been a male custom. In traditional North American cultures, they were a status symbol. In some Pacific cultures, they gave faces a scarier appearance in war. In Papua New Guinea, they are a coming of age symbol.

Lip piercings

In traditional American cultures, only the most important men had lip piercings. In African cultures, lip piercing has generally been a female custom. For the Makololo people of Malawi, it makes a woman more beautiful. For the Saras-Jinjas people of Chad, it indicates that a woman is married. And for the Dogon people of Mali, lip rings have a religious meaning.

Glossary

the Alps (*noun*) – high mountains in Europe

earring (*noun*) – a piece of jewellery that you wear on your ear

pierce (*verb*) – make a cut or hole in something

piercing (*noun*) – a hole in someone's skin for jewellery to fit through

western (*adjective*) – from North America, Europe and Australasia

Life & Style

Writing
Preparing a speech

Reading

1 Read the speech and choose the correct situation.

A scientist is speaking …

a to some Brazilian families.

b to other scientists.

c at the beginning of a new project.

> Good evening. I'd like to say a few words on behalf of the scientists who have come here from Europe.
>
> First of all, I'd like to thank the Environment Research Centre for inviting us to Brazil, and for organising this project so well.
>
> I'd also like to say thank you to our host families. For many of us, this has been our first trip to Brazil, and they have taught us a lot about daily life here during our stay with them.
>
> Thank you, too, for this wonderful meal. We're all sad that our stay in Brazil has ended, but tonight has been a great way to celebrate the things we've done and be with our new friends.
>
> One final thing before I finish. The project has been an opportunity to talk about environmental problems with scientists from around the world and make plans. But there is still a lot of work to do. So, let's continue to work together to save our planet.

2 Read the speech again. Are the sentences true (*T*) or false (*F*)?

1 The speaker is from Brazil. *T / F*

2 He or she is speaking for a group of European scientists. *T / F*

3 The scientists have stayed in hotels. *T / F*

4 They are having dinner together. *T / F*

5 The speaker thinks they have finished their work. *T / F*

Writing skills: organising a speech

3 Put these expressions in the correct order. Then look at the speech again to check your answers.

_____ One final thing before I finish.

_____ First of all, I'd like to thank …

_____ Thank you, too, for …

_____ I'd like to say a few words on behalf of …

_____ So let's continue …

_____ I'd also like to thank …

Language focus: saying thank you

4 Look at the rules. Then correct one mistake in each of the sentences.

Thank	somebody	for	something
Say thank you to			doing something

Thank you	(somebody)	for	something
			doing something

1 Thank you for organise this fantastic party.

2 I'd like to thank all my friends coming this evening.

3 We'd like to say thank to you for all your help.

4 Thank Jack and Tina for travelling all the way from Canada.

Preparing to write

5 Imagine you are going to give a speech for one of these occasions. Make notes for your speech.

a It's the last day of an international conference connected with your work or studies.

b Your family or friends have organised a party to celebrate an important event – your birthday, wedding anniversary, new job or graduation from university.

c An old friend has invited you and a big group of other friends from school to a weekend at his/her house in another country. The friend has paid for flights and organised a big party.

Writing

Write your speech. Use expressions to organise your ideas, and remember to thank people if necessary. Use your notes and the Useful phrases to help you.

Useful phrases

- *I'd like to say a few words / thank everybody on behalf of …*
- *First of all, … Next, … Finally, …*
- *I'd also like to …*
- *Tonight / This meal / This party has been a great way to …*
- *The project / party / meeting has been an opportunity to …*
- *There is still a lot of work to do / food to eat, so let's …*
- *We've been together / known each other for … years.*

Grammar 1A
The -ing form

Complete the sports advice with the correct options.

Regular sport has lots of benefits. You feel better, eat better, and have more energy. (1) *Do / Doing* sport can (2) *help / helping* you sleep better, too. But don't (3) *exercise / exercising* late in the evening because (4) *run / running* and other sports activities wake you up and then you can't (5) *get / getting* to sleep easily. Also, (6) *choose / choosing* the best sport for you is important. (7) *Choose / Choosing* a sport you enjoy. If you like (8) *do / doing* something, it makes you want to continue doing it.

Grammar 1B
The -ing form

Complete the conversation with the correct -*ing* forms in the box

doing	meeting	playing	reading	talking	turning
using	winning				

A: What do you like doing in your free time?

B: I like (1) _____ newspapers and magazines on the internet, and I love (2) _____ to friends on the internet, too. (3) _____ nothing is another one of my favourite activities.

A: I don't like (4) _____ the internet at home. I use it all day at work so I hate (5) _____ on my computer in the house. (6) _____ friends is probably my favourite activity. We play games – cards, board games. We all try to win, but (7) _____ isn't important. We only play for fun.

B: I don't mind (8) _____ board games.

A: Really? Do you want to play Monopoly?

B: OK.

Grammar 2A
going to

Look at the holiday plans for three friends and complete the sentences with *going to*.

	Kim	Jules	Tania
visit a museum	✔	✘	✔
see monuments	✔	✔	✘
watch a football match	✘	✘	✔
eat in a restaurant	✔	✔	✔
swim at the beach	✔	✘	✘
go to the theatre	✔	✘	✔

1 Kim and Tania _____ a museum.

2 Tania _____ monuments.

3 Kim and Jules _____ a football match.

4 The three friends _____ in a restaurant.

5 Kim _____ at the beach.

6 Jules _____ to the theatre.

Grammar 2B
going to

Complete the conversation with the correct form of *going to* and the words in brackets.

Jules: What (1) _____ (you / do) this evening?

Kim: I (2) _____ (watch) TV here. I'm tired.

Jules: (3) _____ (Tania / see) the traditional dancing?

Kim: Yes, she (4) _____. (5) _____ (you / go) with her?

Jules: I don't know. Does it finish late?

Kim: Yes, but she (6) _____ (stay) until the end.

Jules: OK (7) _____ (you / have) dinner in the restaurant tonight?

Kim: No, I (8) _____. I'm not very hungry. I (9) _____ (have) a sandwich here.

Grammar 3A
Present perfect & past simple

Complete the text about the FIFA World Cup with the present perfect or past simple.

The FIFA World Cup™ is one of the world's biggest sports competitions. The first World Cup (1) *has been / was* in Uruguay in 1930, and Uruguay (2) *has won / won* in the final against Argentina. Since then, FIFA (3) *has organised / organised* a World Cup every four years, except in 1942 and 1946. In those years, there (4) *has been / was* no World Cup because of the Second World War. The World Cup (5) *has usually taken / usually took place* in a different continent each time, and FIFA (6) *has selected / selected* countries in five continents to organise it – Asia, Africa, North America, South America and Europe. Brazil (7) *has played / played* in every World Cup – the only team to do this. Many people think the Brazilian team (8) *has played / played* the best football we have ever seen in 1970.

Grammar 3B
Present perfect & past simple

Complete the description with the present perfect or past simple of the verbs in brackets.

My cousin Martina is a really good tennis player. She (1) _____ (start) playing when she was six years old. My uncle (2) _____ (gave) Martina her first lessons and recognised her talent. She's 17 now and she (3) _____ (play) in competitions all over the country. She (4) _____ (not win) any competitions, but last year she (5) _____ (be) in the finals of the national junior competition. She trains really hard, but she (6) _____ (not stop) studying. In fact, she (7) _____ (get) really good results in her exams in June, and she (8) _____ (decide) she wants to go to university. But it's going to be difficult to study and play tennis at the same time.

Vocabulary 1A
Free time activities

Put the activities into the correct column.

| board games | books | cards | comics | newspapers |
| nothing | puzzles | sport | video games | |

do	read	play

Vocabulary 1B
Free time activities

Complete the free time activities in the descriptions.

'In my free time I read (1) b_____. I love reading ghost stories. At the weekend I read two or three (2) n_____ to see what's happening in the world. I also like doing the (3) p_____ – especially Sudoku.'

'I'm very active, so I do (4) s_____ in my free time – football, basketball and other things. When I'm at home I often play (5) v_____ _____ on my computer and I sometimes read (6) c_____. I'm a big Spider-Man fan.'

'I don't like reading or doing sports. In my free time, I sometimes play (7) c_____ with friends. We play a Chinese version of Blackjack. Sometimes we play (8) b_____ _____ too. Our favourite is *Go*. But I also like to sit doing (9) n_____, just watching the world around me.'

Extend your vocabulary 1
fun and *funny*

Complete the conversation with *fun* or *funny*.

A: Did you have (1) _____ at the party?

B: Yeah, it was fantastic! Sania's boyfriend was there. He's really (2) _____. He made everyone laugh. He's been making a film about water sports. He had great (3) _____. He told us about all the (4) _____ things that happened to him. We couldn't stop laughing!

B: So how was your dinner?

A: It was a bit boring. Work dinners are never a lot of (5) _____. But I liked talking to Kim. She's always got lots of (6) _____ stories to tell.

Vocabulary 2A
Places in a city

Match the places in the box to the pictures.

castle   church   shop   airport   sports stadium   market

1 _____

2 _____

3 _____

4 _____

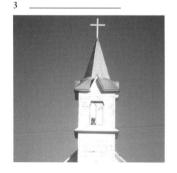

5 _____

6 _____

Vocabulary 2B
Places in a city

Complete the places.

Type of place	Famous examples
1 m_____	The Taj Mahal, India The Parthenon, Greece
2 c_____	The Hagia Sophia, Turkey St. Basil's Cathedral, Russia
3 a_____ g_____	The Louvre, France The Museum of Modern Art, US
4 c_____	Castel del Monte, Italy Himeji C..., Japan
5 m_____	Portobello, UK The Souks, Morroco
6 b_____	Daytona, US Copacobana, Brazil
7 m_____	The Egyptian M..., Egypt. The Natural History M..., UK
8 s_____ s_____	The Bird's Nest, China Estadio Azteca, Mexico
9 t_____	La Scala, Milan, Italy Sydney Opera House, Australia

Vocabulary 3A
Sports

Write the name of the sport. Add *-ball* or *-ing* to the words in the box. Check your spelling!

basket	cycle	foot	run	ski	volley

1 _____

3 _____   4 _____

5 _____   6 _____

Vocabulary 3B
Sports

Choose *go* or *play* to complete the list of activities. Circle your answers.

Come to the Mountain Sports Resort.

At the resort you can …

1 *go / play* tennis.
2 *go / play* golf in the summer.
3 *go / play* skiing in the winter.
4 *go / play* basketball.
5 *go / play* swimming all year.
6 *go / play* football.
7 *go / play* running.
8 *go / play* cycling.
9 *go / play* volleyball.

Extend your vocabulary 2
-less, -ful

Complete the conversation with the correct words.

A: Did you know I hurt my back playing basketball?

B: No, I didn't.

A: I was very (1) *careless / careful*. It was my first game in years, and I didn't do any exercises to prepare for it. The sports centre called a doctor. It was very (2) *painless / painful*. Anyway, I went to a special hospital last week and it was really (3) *helpless / helpful*. I was worried before I went, but it was fantastic. The people there were very (4) *careless / careful*, and the treatment was completely (5) *painless / painful*. And the hospital's in a really (6) *beautyful / beautiful* place in the middle of the mountains.

Vocabulary 4
Playing games

Complete the conversation with the words and phrases in the box.

cheating	lose	objective	points	turn	win

A: Let's play pool.

B: OK. How do you play?

A: The (1) _____ is to put all your balls in the holes.

B: The balls have numbers. Are they (2) _____?

A: No. You (3) _____ the game if you put the black ball in a hole after your balls. But you (4) _____ if you hit the black ball into a hole before your balls. You start.

B: Me? OK.

A: You hit the white ball twice. That's (5) _____.

B: I didn't know!

A: It's my (6) _____ now, and I get two turns because you cheated.

Pronunciation
Word bingo

🔘 **1.29** Listen and circle the words you hear.

1	see	she
2	take	took
3	phone	phoned
4	your	you
5	hair	air
6	three	tree
7	hear	her
8	boat	vote
9	sports	sport
10	gave	game

Listening
Music and exercising

🔘 **1.30** Listen to a news story and choose the best answers to the questions.

1 Can music make you run faster?
   a Yes, it can.
   b No, it can't.

2 What type of music is good when you are training?
   a Every type of music.
   b The right type of music.

3 Can music make you stronger?
   a Yes, it can.
   b No, it can't, but you feel stronger.

4 Is exercising with music good for all of us?
   a No, just for professional sports people.
   b Yes – it makes exercising more fun.

5 Does the interviewer listen to music when she goes running?
   a No, but she's going to listen to music next time.
   b Yes, she does.

6 Do all sportspeople use music when they are preparing for a competition?
   a Yes, they do. It helps them to concentrate.
   b No, they don't. Some sportspeople can't concentrate with music.

Reading
Chess

1 What do you think? Choose one option in each sentence.

1 Chess *is / isn't* a very old game.
2 It *is / isn't* popular all around the world.
3 World chess champions *have / haven't* come from many different countries.
4 Computers *can / can't* play chess well.

2 Read the article and check your answers to exercise 1.

3 Read the article again and answer the questions.

1 Why do some countries want to have a world chess champion?

_____

_____

2 Where did chess start?

_____

_____

3 Where does the word *chess* come from?

_____

_____

4 Where did the modern rules develop?

_____

_____

5 What do you need to decide before your next turn in a chess game?

_____

_____

6 What's the connection between chess and video games?

_____

_____

7 Why were computer scientists interested in chess?

_____

_____

4 Test your memory. What happened at these times or dates? Read the article again to check your answers.

1 10th century

_____

2 1851

_____

3 1886

_____

4 1997

_____

5 Find in the article:

1 three examples of the present perfect:

_____, _____, _____

2 two synonyms for world:

_____, _____

3 two superlatives:

_____, _____

4 an *-ing* form after a preposition:

_____

5 *going to* for a personal intention:

_____

6 the opposite of lost:

_____

6 Complete the text with the correct form of the verbs in brackets.

In the past, the best players of games (a) _____ (be) human. But in recent years computers (b) _____ (learn) to play many games well, including chess. (c) _____ (play) cards well still gives computers problems, but computer scientists say they (d) _____ (find) solutions for these problems soon. We humans like (e) _____ (win), but it's clear that in the future computers (f) _____ (win) every game we play against them.

The original brain training game

Since its origins about 1,500 years ago, chess has become one of the world's most popular games. Hundreds of millions of people play it in homes, cafés and clubs around the globe. Children play at schools to help them think better. And having a world chess champion shows the rest of the planet that a country has power.

History

Exactly where chess started isn't clear, but from India it travelled to Persia (Iran today). Players lose the game when they lose their king, and the English name, chess, comes from shāh, the Persian word for king. From Persia, chess travelled to the Islamic world. It arrived in southern Europe in about the 10th century, and the modern rules developed there.

The first modern chess tournament was in London in 1851, and the first official World Champion was the Austrian-American Wilhelm Steinitz in 1886. Since then, there have been champions from Germany, Cuba, France, Russia, Latvia, Georgia, the United States and India.

The game

For centuries, people have seen chess as a good way to prepare for making decisions in life. That's because chess is an excellent combination of strategy – making a plan for a complete game – and tactics – deciding what you are going to do next. Today, we buy video games to make our brains younger, but chess is the original brain training game.

A digital champion

The game changed for ever at the end of the 20th century. For computer scientists, chess was the perfect way to test their computers. Until 1997, computers always lost in games against humans. But in that year, the computer Deep Blue played the world champion Garry Kasparov ... and won. The best player in the world was a computer.

10 Fun & Games

Writing
Writing an email

Reading

1 Read the email. Is it formal or informal?

```
○ ○ ○
```

Hi Lou,

How's it going in Sydney? I'm sending this email from our hotel in New Delhi, India. It's really hot and Manu's having a nap.

So far we've had a great time. We've seen the Taj Mahal, and that was amazing. I can see why it's one of the New Seven Wonders of the World.

We plan to visit some cities in Rajasthan next. We're going to Jaipur by train tomorrow, and we'd like to go to Udaipur too. John went there last year and he really recommended it. Do you have his email address, by the way?

What about you? Have you decided where to go for your holidays? Let me know your plans.

Anyway, I must go. We're going to walk around the old city this afternoon and visit the Red Fort. Then I want to go to bed early. We've got a long day tomorrow!

Take care,

Jess

2 Read the email again and complete the information.

From (1) _____ in (2) _____

to (3) _____ in (4) _____

Things Jess has done: (5) _____

_____

Plans for today: (6) _____

_____

Other plans: (7) _____

_____

Writing skills: common expressions in informal emails

3 Write the words and expressions for starting and ending emails in the correct column.

```
All the best,   Hi …   Dear …   Take care,   Love,
Best wishes,
```

At the start	At the end

4 Find the expressions in the box in the email. Then complete the email below with the expressions.

```
anyway   by the way   how's it going   let me know
what about you
```

Hi Myrna

(1) _____? We're having a great time in Madagascar. (2) _____? Are you enjoying your holiday?

I'm going to have my birthday party on 24th, (3) _____. When are you going to be back in Cape Town? (4) _____ and I can come to meet you at the airport.

(5) _____, I must stop. We're going out for dinner and we're going to be late if we don't leave now!

Love,

Sam

Language focus: talking about plans

5 Complete the plans from the email.

1 We _____ some cities in Rajasthan next.

2 We _____ Jaipur by train tomorrow.

3 We _____ around the old city this afternoon.

Fun & Games

Preparing to write

6 Imagine you are on holiday. Make notes about things you are doing, things you have done and your plans.

Writing

Write an email to a friend telling them about your holiday. Use your notes and the Useful phrases to help you.

Useful phrases

- *How's it going / How are things in …*
- *I'm writing / sending this e-card in / from …*
- *I'm having a great / fantastic time.*
- *The weather's great / terrible.*
- *So far, / Until now, I've …*
- *Tomorrow, / This afternoon/evening, / At the weekend, …*
- *I'm going to*
- *I plan / I intend to …*
- *I'd like*

Audioscript

Unit 1

Vocabulary 6

1 peter@jsmail.com
2 sally@sallysmith.co.uk
3 www.kimwebb.com/index.htm
4 www3.factsandfigures.net
5 www.newscientist.com/section/space

Pronunciation 1

1 A J H K
2 E P V G B T C D
3 L X Z S M L F
4 I Y
5 U W Q

Pronunciation 2

1 A: My name's Joy.
   B: How do you spell that?
   A: J-O-Y
2 A: My name's Ted
   B: How do you spell that?
   A: T-E-D
3 A: My name's Zoe
   B: How do you spell that?
   A: Z-O-E
4 A: My name's Xavi.
   B: How do you spell that?
   A: X-A-V-I
5 A: My name's Wilma
   B: How do you spell that?
   A: W-I-L-M-A
6 A: My name's Faruq
   B: How do you spell that?
   A: F-A-R-U-Q
7 A: My name's Becky
   B: How do you spell that?
   A: B-E-C-K-Y
8 A: My name's Pasha
   B: How do you spell that?
   A: P-A-S-H-A

Listening

Hello, and welcome to our first talk about the English language and its history. Today, Doctor Susan Fielding is here to talk about the English alphabet. For more information about the talks, you can visit our website. Doctor Fielding …

Good evening. Let's start with a definition. What is an alphabet? The letters in an alphabet are consonants and vowels in a particular language. The English alphabet has 26 letters. The problem is, English has 40 consonants and vowels! That's 14 consonants and vowels that *aren't* in the alphabet. To solve this problem, English uses a combination of letters for the 14 extra consonants and vowels. For example, *s h* represents the consonant 'sh', and *c h* represents the consonant 'ch'.

The English alphabet is, in fact, the same as the Latin alphabet. And the Latin alphabet we use today comes from the Greek alphabet. The English word *alphabet* comes from the Greek word *alphabetos*, and this word is a combination of the first two letters of the Greek alphabet – *alpha* and *beta*. *Alpha … beta … alpha … bet.*

Audioscript

Unit 2

Vocabulary 6B

1 Monday 10th May
2 Wednesday 15th June
3 Saturday 2nd August
4 Thursday 30th November
5 Sunday 3rd March
6 Tuesday 21st February
7 Friday 5th July

Pronunciation 1

1 Russian
2 Italian
3 American
4 Chinese
5 Scottish
6 Swedish
7 Vietnamese
8 Japanese

Pronunciation 2

1 He gets to work at 8.
2 Here are your keys.
3 She finishes work at 6.
4 He has lunch at work.
5 Three buses go to the centre.
6 Where are my books?
7 These are easy exercises.
8 I remember school dinners.

Listening

A: Hello, and welcome to the travel show. Today, we're talking to Miriam Masekela about global cities. Miriam, you're from Johannesburg in South Africa. Is your city a global city?

B: Yes, it is.

A: And what *is* a global city? Is it the same as a megacity?

B: No, it isn't. They are different things. Megacities have more than ten million inhabitants. Global cities are important to the economy of the world.

A: How many global cities are there?

B: It's a difficult question because there isn't one definition of a global city. But if you look at lists of global cities, the first two are usually London and New York. Then we have cities like Beijing, Hong Kong, Tokyo, Paris and Sydney.

A: And what are the characteristics of a global city?

B: First of all, global cities are the location of a lot of international corporations and institutions. That's very important. But there are other characteristics too. Transport, for example. Global cities have an international airport, and an advanced transport system. They also have important universities and museums. And people *know* their names. I say Tokyo, and you immediately know where it is.

Audioscript

Unit 3

Pronunciation 1

1 A: Where are you from?
    B: I'm from Milan in Italy.

2 A: What's Milan like?
    B: It's very big.

3 A: Do you have a big family?
    B: Yes, I do.

4 A: Are you married?
    B: Yes, I am.

5 A: What's your husband's name?
    B: Mehmet.

6 A: Does he come from Italy?
    B: No, he doesn't. He's Turkish.

7 A: Do you live in Milan now?
    B: No we don't. We live in Turkey.

Pronunciation 2

1 A: Does Marcus like football?
    B: Football? He hates it.

2 A: Do you like rap music?
    B: Rap music? I love it.

3 A: What do you think of dogs?
    B: Dogs? I like them.

4 A: Does Myrna like coffee?
    B: Coffee? She hates it.

5 A: What's your opinion of shopping?
    B: Shopping? I like it.

6 A: Do your grandparents like computers?
    B: Computers? They love them.

Listening

A: Hi! I'm at the World of Music and Dance festival in England. I want to find out who comes here and why. Excuse me, what's your name?

B: Jo.

A: Why do you come here?

B: Because I like music from different countries. And because it's easy to come here with kids, and I've got three!

A: So this isn't your first time here?

B: No, it's my … sixth time.

A: And what's your name?

C: Misha.

A: Do you come every year?

C: No, it's my first time.

A: And why are you here?

C: I'm here to play. My group plays traditional Russian music.

A: And do you like the festival?

C: Yes, it's nice. But it's noisy at night. I can't sleep.

A: Excuse me. What's your name?

D: Yara.

A: And why are you here?

D: It's a good place to meet my friends. I have friends in different places and we meet here for three days. In the morning we talk. In the afternoon and evening we listen to music and dance.

A: And who do you want to see?

D: There's a very good Nigerian group here, and another from Russia.

A: Well, thanks for speaking to us.

D: You're welcome.

Audioscript

Unit 4

Pronunciation 1

1 Is this your grandfather's house?
2 His dog's very friendly.
3 Does it sleep outdoors in the square?
4 Is there a lamp in this room?
5 There's one on the shelf near that armchair.
6 There's a fridge in his bathroom!

Pronunciation 2

1 Camel's milk is very nice.
2 Feta? It's a sort of cheese.
3 Brownies are cakes.
4 Ciabatta is a type of bread.
5 Fish is good for you.
6 Does Rajiv want a cup of tea?
7 Basmati? It's a kind of rice.
8 Do the children want a glass of milk?

Listening

A: Oui, allô?
B: Er … hello. I'm phoning about the house exchange.
A: Ah, hello.
B: Can I ask you some questions?
A: Of course.
B: What's the village like?
A: It's very small and beautiful – you can see the mountains from the house. It's busy in the winter, but quiet in July and August.
B: Are there any shops in the village?
A: Yes, there is a small supermarket.
B: And is it easy to get to a town?
A: The nearest town is about 50 minutes by bus. The train station is there. But there aren't many buses.
B: Can we get a taxi from the station?
A: Yes, it's the best option.
B: And what about the house?
A: It's quite big – we have three bedrooms.
B: I need to check emails. Do you have an Internet connection?
A: Yes, we do. And we have cable television. You can watch TV in English.
B: And what about kids? Are there things for children to do?

A: Oh, yes. I have two children. Do your children like video games?
B: Yes.
A: We have video games, DVDs, games, books. And there is a park for children to play in, in the village.
B: Well, that sounds great. What would you like to know about our house?
A: Where is it exactly?

Audioscript

Unit 5

Pronunciation 1

1 rich
2 leave
3 steal
4 live
5 eat
6 his
7 it
8 he's
9 reach
10 still

Pronunciation 2

1 Can you turn up the radio?
2 Please sit down.
3 Don't turn off the computer!
4 We stand up when the teacher comes in.
5 Turn down that TV!
6 Sit down and listen to me.
7 Turn off the television. It's time to go to bed.

Listening

A: So, Mei, what's today's question for our listeners?

B: Our question today is what type of films do you like? Do you like Hollywood films or do you prefer other types of films?

A: What do you prefer, Mei?

B: I don't watch Hollywood films very often. I prefer independent films.

A: Why's that?

B: Because they have new ideas, they're different. I like world cinema, too. You can see how other people around the world live and how they see the world. I love listening to other languages too. What about you?

A: I prefer Hollywood films.

B: Really? Why?

A: Because I go to the cinema to relax and Hollywood films are fun. Independent films are sometimes a bit sad and serious.

B: But Hollywood doesn't have any new ideas! Hollywood films just copy old films or independent films. Take *Vanilla Sky*, for example. The original Spanish film's really good. The Hollywood version's boring.

A: But it's got famous actors in it! Hollywood films are spectacular, they're exciting. And they have my favourite actors.

B: Well I like seeing new actors.

A: So, do you want to go to the cinema later?

B: No I don't. Not with you!

Audioscript

Unit 6

Pronunciation 1

1 I can't understand this. It's in Japanese.
2 Can you read Japanese?
3 No, I cant.
4 But Jorgen can speak Japanese
5 Can you give me his number?
6 Yes, I can. It's in my diary.

Pronunciation 2

1 physics
2 languagc
3 teacher
4 pencil
5 English
6 hotel
7 doctor
8 lawyer
9 thriller
10 cartoon
11 August
12 July

Listening

A: On today's programme, we look at home schooling with Karl Lavinsky. Karl, what *is* home schooling?
B: Home schooling is when children don't go to school. They have lessons at home, usually with a parent, but sometimes with a teacher.
A: And why do people choose home schooling?
B: There are a number of reasons. One is about the type of education children get in schools. In general, children who learn at home get better test results. Also, some parents aren't happy with traditional education. Some think schools are unfriendly, others are unhappy with the things they teach at school. It can also be a practical decision. When I was a child, the nearest school was 50 kilometres from my house. Learning at home was the only option. Or maybe a family goes to live in another country, and wants to continue with the school programme from home.
A: And is home schooling just an American thing?
B: No, it isn't. It's an option in Canada, Australia, New Zealand, the UK and some other European countries too.

A: One final question. What about the social life in schools – making friends, meeting different people?
B: I think if parents choose home schooling, it's important for their children to meet other children outside of the home, at sports clubs, music lessons, etc.

Audioscript

Unit 7

Pronunciation 1

1 I visited Hanoi.
2 I stayed at a hotel.
3 I wanted to see an old friend.
4 I looked for his number.
5 I picked up the phone.
6 I phoned his number.
7 I waited.
8 The answer phone started.
9 I listened to the message.
10 The message ended.
11 I decided to leave a message.
12 He called me the next day.

Pronunciation 2

1 Who did William see on Wednesday?
2 Where does Wendy work?
3 When was the weather windy?
4 When was William in Winchester?
5 How many hours do you have to help me?
6 Who did Henry have lunch with?

Listening

A: Today in Consumer Views I'm out on the streets to ask people where they get their news. Excuse me … Where do you get your news?
B: I read the newspaper on the internet at work, and I watch the news on TV every night. I sometimes listen to the radio too.
A: And did you read a newspaper this morning?
B: No, I didn't. I didn't have time.
A: Excuse me. Can I ask you a question? Where do you get your news?
C: I'm not interested in the news.
A: Why's that?
C: It's all negative, and we can't change anything. I just turn the TV on at the end of the news to watch the sports results and the weather.
A: So what do you watch on TV?
C: Documentaries and sports programmes mainly.
A: Do you have a moment? Where do you get your news?
D: I usually put the radio on in the car when I travel to work.

A: Do you ever buy a newspaper?
D: No, I don't. I sometimes get the train to work and read one of those free newspapers.
A: Did you read a paper this morning?
D: Yes, I did.

Audioscript

Unit 8

Pronunciation 1

1 England's in the United Kingdom.
2 They're having a meeting in Singapore.
3 I think there's something in the fridge.
4 We're watching a boring film.
5 This evening we want to sing in a karaoke bar.
6 He's travelling to China by train.

Pronunciation 2

1 Is it true that the Reeds have moved?
2 Yes, they have.
3 Where did they go to?
4 They went to Spain.
5 I hope you can contact them.
6 Yes, I can.
7 Here's the address.
8 And here's the phone number they left.

Listening

A: Hello, and welcome to *Any Questions*? Our first question today is from Mr Alatas from Indonesia. He writes 'I'm starting to travel a lot on business. Do you have any advice for long flights?'

B: There are two problems here. The long flight, and the time difference between your home and the destination. First, the flight. When you're spending hours on a plane, you need to move. You can sit and do exercises in your seat, but it's good if you also stand up and walk a little. Also, choose your seat well. On cheaper flights you normally don't have much space, so book a seat next to an emergency exit. They've got more space. And remember to drink lots of water or fruit juice. In fact, it's good to drink plenty of water *before* your flight. That way, you don't need to go to the toilet so often on the plane. Don't drink coffee or tea.

A: What about the time difference?

B: It's a difficult problem. For example when you arrive, it's time for bed at home. But at your destination it's morning. One idea is to change the time on your watch to the time at your destination. If possible, sleep when the people at your destination are sleeping.

Unit 9

Pronunciation

1 You can't wear shorts with socks!
2 June normally wears a skirt and a shirt to work.
3 I see you have short hair now.
4 Have a shower before you swim.
5 My sisters are in a talent show.
6 I need to x-ray your stomach and your shoulder.

Listening

A: Hello. On today's show we have Andrea Becker. She works in the ecotourist industry. Andrea, what *is* an ecotourist?

B: Traditional tourists usually visit cities or go to the beach. Ecotourists visit the natural world, and want to see unusual animals and plants.

A: Right.

B: Also, all tourists, including ecotourists, change the places they visit, and these changes are often negative for the local people and environment. But ecotourists try to *protect* the local environment, and *help* local people. Our groups of tourists are small, and a lot of the money we earn goes to the local economy.

A: You organise trips around the world. What countries have you been to?

B: A lot of countries, but the most popular destination is Costa Rica because it has so many unusual plant and animal species.

A: Is the ecotourist industry getting bigger?

B: Yes, it is. The tourist industry in general is growing, but the ecotourist industry has grown about 10 percent recently.

A: Has this created problems?

B: Yes, it has. A lot of traditional tourist companies want to make money from ecotourists. Some use the word 'ecotourist' to sell holidays that aren't good for the environment or for local people. They organise big groups, and most of the money goes to the tourist company, not to the local economy.

A: Andrea, thank you for talking to us.

B: You're welcome.

Audioscript

Unit 10

Pronuncation 1

1 she
2 take
3 phoned
4 you
5 hair
6 three
7 her
8 boat
9 sports
10 game

Listening

A: Next, Jade Whiting brings us a report about sport and music. Jade.

B: The objective of professional sport is to win, and we all understand the importance of exercise and eating well. But there's a third thing to consider, and that's music. Yes, it's official – the right music can make you run faster!

Sports scientists have demonstrated that music has an important role in preparing for a competition. Their experiments show that if you listen to the right music when you are training, you can train harder and you feel better when you finish. Listening to the right music before doing a sport can also make you stronger.

A lot of professionals from all sports now use music to help them prepare for competitions. But the music connection is good news for all of us. We all know that doing some exercise is important, but many of us don't like doing it. Listening to music can make exercise more fun, and help people to continue doing it. I'm certainly going to try listening to music when I go running tonight!

But not all sports people are positive. One Olympic sportsman said that he needed to concentrate before a competition, and music made that impossible.

Answer Key

Unit 1

Grammar 1

1 a **2** an **3** an **4** a **5** an **6** a

Grammar 2

1 computers	4 universities
2 Windows	5 buses
3 families	6 sandwiches

Grammar 3A

1 're	5 aren't
2 's	6 're
3 'm	7 Are you
4 isn't	8 Is it

Grammar 3B

1 Are	4 isn't
2 aren't	5 Are
3 Is	6 am

Grammar 4A

1 your	4 our
2 My	5 Their
3 his	6 Its

Grammar 4B

1 Their	4 her
2 Your	5 your
3 my	6 our

Vocabulary 1

1 radio	4 love
2 family	5 golf
3 kilometre	

Vocabulary 2

Across	Down
2 doctor	1 zoo
5 question	3 radio
7 x-ray	4 menu
8 family	6 email

Vocabulary 3

1 ten	6 two
2 six	7 five
3 four	8 eight
4 one	9 three
5 nine	10 seven

Vocabulary 4A

1 ✔
2 ✘ - The correct answer is 31 (thirty-one).
3 ✔
4 ✘ - The correct answer is 18 (eighteen).
5 ✘ - The correct answer is 90 (ninety)
6 ✔

Vocabulary 4B

1 twenty-three	5 thirty-seven
2 fourteen	6 fifty-five
3 forty-six	7 twelve
4 eighteen	8 eighty-nine

Vocabulary 5A

1 first	4 fifth
2 tenth	5 eighth
3 third	6 second

Vocabulary 5B

1 sixth	6 eighth
2 seventh	7 tenth
3 first	8 second
4 forty-fourth	9 fifth
5 third	10 ninth

Extend your vocabulary

1 about 4	4 5
2 1	5 53
3 about 50	6 353

Vocabulary 6

1 a **2** b **3** a **4** a **5** b

Pronunciation 1

1 b **2** e **3** c **4** a **5** d

Pronunciation 2

1 Joy	5 Wilma
2 Ted	6 Faruq
3 Zoe	7 Becky
4 Xavi	8 Pasha

Listening

1 the English alphabet	4 aren't
2 26	5 the same
3 40	6 Greek

Reading

1
1 27
2 8,850m
3 192, 193, 194 or 195
2
The student's own answers.
3
1 the internet
2 in a library
3 1999
4 the Vatican City, Kosovo and Taiwan
5 compare information from different websites.
4
1 c **2** a **3** b **4** e **5** d
5

1 is	4 aren't / are not
2 is	5 is
3 are	

Writing

1
1 She needs English at work.
2 On the internet with a webcam, or by Messenger, email or letter.
3 Her postcode and telephone number.
4 Her job and her marital status (she's single).
2
1 c **2** a **3** d **4** f **5** b **6** e
3

1 Paragraph 3	5 Paragraph 1
2 Paragraph 2	6 Paragraph 1
3 Paragraph 1	7 Paragraph 1
4 Paragraph 3	

4
The student's own answers

Answer Key

Unit 2

Grammar 1A

1 from	**4** from
2 in	**5** in
3 near	

Grammar 1B

1 in	**4** near
2 from	**5** in
3 in	**6** in

The name of the city is Strasbourg.

Grammar 2A

1 What is your home town?
2 Why is it famous?
3 How old is the Taj Mahal?
4 Where is Agra?
5 What is it like?
6 When is a good time to visit?

Grammar 2B

1 Where	**4** What
2 How old	**5** Why
3 What	**6** When

Grammar 3A

1 gets	**4** has
2 goes	**5** finishes
3 starts	**6** watches

Grammar 3B

1 finishes	**4** have
2 get up	**5** goes
3 go	**6** opens

Grammar 4A

1 doesn't have	**4** doesn't work
2 don't celebrate	**5** don't go
3 doesn't open	**6** don't get

Grammar 4B

1 don't have	**4** doesn't follow
2 doesn't take	**5** don't add
3 doesn't have	**6** doesn't use

Vocabulary 1

1 American	**6** Mexican
2 Brazilian	**7** Polish
3 Chinese	**8** Turkish
4 German	**9** Russian
5 Japanese	**10** Vietnamese

Vocabulary 2

Across	Down
2 Czech	**1** German
5 French	**3** Dutch
6 Polish	**4** Thai

Vocabulary 3A

1 c **2** a **3** d **4** b

Vocabulary 3B

1 old	**4** modern
2 busy	**5** noisy
3 quiet	

Extend your vocabulary

1 It's very noisy too.
2 It's also a conference centre.
3 I'm also Basque.
4 We're students too.
5 They speak good English too.
6 It's also quiet.

Vocabulary 4A

1 have	**4** go
2 get	**5** have
3 have	

Vocabulary 4B

1 up	**5** lunch
2 have	**6** go
3 go	**7** home
4 get	**8** bed

Vocabulary 5

1 months	**4** seconds
2 years	**5** minutes
3 decades	**6** hours

Vocabulary 6A

1 Saturday, Sunday	**5** Wednesday
2 January	**6** July, August
3 Monday	**7** February
4 November, September	**8** October

Vocabulary 6B

1 Monday 10th May
2 Wednesday 15th June
3 Saturday 2nd August
4 Thursday 30th November
5 Sunday 3rd March
6 Tuesday 21st February
7 Friday 5th July

Pronunciation 1

1 a	**5** a
2 b	**6** a
3 b	**7** c
4 b	**8** c

Pronunciation 2

1 /s/	**5** /ɪz/
2 /z/	**6** /s/
3 /ɪz/	**7** /ɪz/
4 /z/	**8** /z/

Listening

1 global city	**5** airport
2 New York	**6** transport
3 Tokyo	**7** universities
4 institutions	

Reading

1
Student's own answers
2
1 b **2** c **3** a
3
1 In China, Japan, South Asia, North Africa and southern Europe.
2 A 30-minute nap.
3 Because people sometimes have a negative opinion of siestas (because if you sleep you don't work).
4 It gives you more energy, and you can concentrate more.
5 $23.50 ($14 + $9.50)
6 20 to 30 minutes
4
1 full of
2 tired
3 concentrate
4 example, company
5

1 need	**5** has
2 don't sleep	**6** doesn't take
3 work	**7** work
4 doesn't finish	

Writing

1
2
2

1 5pm / 5 o'clock	**5** 1.30pm
2 4pm / 4 o'clock	**6** 6pm / 6 o'clock
3 5:30pm	**7** 11pm
4 5pm / 5 o'clock	

3

1 at	**4** during
2 from, to	**5** before
3 until	**6** after

4
1 typically, normally
2 typical
3 A lot of

Answer Key

Unit 3

Grammar 1A
1 brother's
2 girlfriend's
3 cousins'
4 mother's
5 children's
6 parents'

Grammar 1B
1 cousin's father
2 grandparents' parents
3 Laos' capital city
4 uncle's children
5 the world's most popular
6 sister's name

Grammar 2A
1 Does   4 do   7 Do
2 does   5 do   8 don't
3 Do   6 don't

Grammar 2B
1 Do you have
2 Does your brother visit
3 Do both your parents work
4 Does your father have
5 Do you use
6 Do your grandparents live

Grammar 3A
1 Where do Tom and Greg meet
2 Why do they go
3 What do they do
4 When does Tom get
5 Why do you ask

Grammar 3B
1 Where do you go shopping?
2 When does the market open?
3 Why do people like video games?
4 What does mall mean?
5 Where do people play basketball?
6 When does February have 20 days?

Grammar 4A
1 her   4 us   7 it
2 him   5 me   8 you
3 them   6 you

Grammar 4B
1 him   3 her   5 you
2 them   4 us   6 it

Vocabulary 1A

Male	Female	Male and female
brother	wife	children
father	daughter	cousin
son	mother	

husband	sister	
grandfather	aunt	
uncle	granddaughter	

Vocabulary 1B
1 brother   7 wife
2 sister   8 son
3 mother   9 husband
4 father   10 children
5 grandmother   11 grandson
6 cousins   12 granddaughter

Vocabulary 2
1 black   6 orange
2 white   7 blue
3 grey   8 green
4 red   9 brown
5 yellow

Vocabulary 3A
1 c   2 f   3 d   4 b   5 a   6 e

Vocabulary 3B
1 up   5 go to
2 play   6 a lot
3 about   7 in
4 go shopping 8 see

Vocabulary 4A
1 ugly   4 dirty
2 unfriendly 5 stupid
3 awful

Vocabulary 4B
1 friendly   4 intelligent
2 nice   5 clean
3 beautiful

Extend your vocabulary
1 I really hate cats.
2 This is a really noisy city.
3 We really love our car.
4 London's parks are really beautiful.
5 Horses are really friendly animals
6 My sister really likes shopping.

Pronunciation 1
1
1 ↘   2 ↘   3 ↗   4 ↗   5 ↘   6 ↗   7 ↗
2
Intonation rises in Yes/No questions.

Pronunciation 2
1
1 hates   4 hates
2 love   5 like
3 like   6 love
2
a

Listening

	Jo	Misha	Yara
1			✔
2		✔	
3	✔		
4		✔	
5	✔		✔
6		✔	

Reading
1
1 The students' own answer.
2 Five best friends and another ten good friends.
2
1 social networking
2 anthropologist
3 friend, place in your social world
4 number, possible
5 meet 150 friends regularly
3
1 Facebook has more than 200 million users.
2 Facebook users have about 120 friends.
3 150 is the maximum number of friends a person can have.
4
1 acquaintances
2 According to
3 close
4 That seems about right to me.
5
1 them   4 her
2 us   5 me
3 them   6 it

Writing
1
1 friend
2 aunt and uncle
3 cousins
2
1 James
2 Nick's aunt and her family
3 Elsie and Kevin
4 Tom and Barbara
5 Elsie, Kevin, Tom and Barbara
6 Elsie, Kevin, Tom and Barbara
3
1 They both like football.
2 They're all on holiday.
3 They all stay in touch by email.
4 They both go to school in Glasgow.

Answer Key

Unit 4

Grammar 1A
1 are
2 are
3 is
4 isn't
5 isn't
6 aren't

Grammar 1B
1 is there
2 there is
3 Are there
4 there are
5 Is there
6 there isn't
7 Are there
8 There are

Grammar 2A
1 some
2 an
3 some
4 some
5 an
6 some
7 some
8 a

Grammar 2B
1 Correct
2 Incorrect – Use no article + uncountable noun (bread)
3 Correct
4 Correct
5 Incorrect – Use an + singular countable noun (an apple) OR some + plural countable noun (some apples)
6 Incorrect – Use some + uncountable noun (some toast), OR no article + uncountable noun (toast)
7 Correct
8 Incorrect – Use some + uncountable noun (some fruit), OR no article + uncountable noun (fruit)

Grammar 3A
1 a lot of
2 many
3 much
4 some
5 some
6 much
7 many
8 some

Grammar 3B
1 don't eat much / don't eat a lot of
2 have a lot of
3 cooks some
4 doesn't prepare much / doesn't prepare a lot of
5 aren't many
6 eat a lot of

Vocabulary 1A
1 b 2 f 3 g 4 a 5 h 6 c 7 e 8 d

Vocabulary 1B
1 transfer
2 park
3 room
4 access
5 gym
6 pool
7 bar
8 restaurant
9 tours
10 cable

Vocabulary 2A

Kitchen	Living room	Bathroom
cooker	couch/sofa	bath
fridge		shower
		toilet

Bedroom	In two or more rooms
wardrobe	cupboard
	lamp
	armchair
	shelf

Vocabulary 2B
1 bath
2 shower
3 toilet
4 cooker
5 fridge
6 cupboard
7 armchair
8 couch, sofa
9 shelf
10 a wardrobe
11 a lamp

Vocabulary 3A

Dairy products	Drinks	Fruit	Other things
cheese	a cup of	oranges	rice
butter	tea	bananas	fish
eggs	milk		bread
	juice		jam
	coffee		cakes

Vocabulary 3B
1 fish
2 rice
3 jam
4 cakes
5 cheese
6 milk

Extend your vocabulary
1 Darjeeling is a type of tea.
2 Marmalade is a sort of jam.
3 Cappuccino is a kind of coffee.
4 A dictionary is a kind of book.
5 Motels are a sort of hotel.
6 A taxi is a type of transport.

Vocabulary 4

Across
2 rice
5 crisps
7 tomatoes
8 carrots
9 beans

Down
1 pizza
3 chips
4 meat
6 potatoes

Pronunciation 1
1 grandfather
2 friendly
3 outdoors, square
4 lamp
5 shelf, armchair
6 fridge, bathroom

Pronunciation 2
1 Camel's milk is very nice.
2 Feta? It's a sort of cheese.
3 Brownies are cakes.
4 Ciabatta is a type of bread.
5 Fish is good for you.
6 Does Rajiv want a cup of tea?
7 Basmati? It's a kind of rice.
8 Do the children want a glass of milk?

Listening
1 b 2 c 3 a 4 b 5 a 6 c

Reading
1
The student's own answers.
2
1 True
2 False – about 30% of people in India don't eat any meat.
3 True
4 True
3

	Meat	Fish	Cheese and eggs
Semi-vegetarians	No	Yes	Yes
Vegetarians	No	No	Yes
Vegans	No	No	No

4
1 many, Four
2 much, 8 kilos
3 many, between 3 and 7%
4 often, One day a week / Every week
5
1 much
2 a lot of
3 some
4 any
5 many
6 a lot of

Writing
1
b
2
He asks about:
Number of bedrooms? ✔
Near centre? ✔
Buses? ✔
Address? ✔
Price? ✔
When available? ✔
3
1 Are
2 Could
3 Do
4 Is
5 Does
6 Could
4
The missing question word is How.
1 c 2 a 3 d 4 b

Answer Key

Unit 5

Grammar 1A

1 e 2 d 3 f 4 a 5 b 6 c

Grammar 1B

1 We go to the cinema three times a month.
2 We watch a film on TV every two days.
3 We watch DVDs about twice a month.
4 We download a film every week.
5 I read film reviews four or five times a week.
6 I read them about once a year!

Grammar 2A

always often sometimes not often never

Grammar 2B

1 I don't often watch television.
2 There are always sports programmes on, and I hate sport!
3 I sometimes watch films, but only once or twice a week.
4 I am never at home when my favourite programmes are on.
5 I often read about interesting documentaries in the TV guide.
6 But they are often on late at night.
7 I always get up very early.
8 I sometimes stay up late to watch a documentary, though.

Grammar 2C

1 We always watch the news.
2 Tom doesn't often watch football.
3 We often buy a newspaper.
4 I sometimes cycle to work when the weather is nice.
5 I am often home at five o'clock.
6 There are always good programmes on TV after work.
7 I never watch television. I don't have a TV.

Vocabulary 1A

1 on	5 film
2 review	6 at, back
3 cinema	7 in, middle
4 ticket	

Vocabulary 2

1 see	4 go
2 read	5 sit
3 buy	6 watch

Vocabulary 3A

1 horror	4 science fiction
2 romantic drama	5 cartoon
3 thriller	

Vocabulary 3B

1 c 2 a 3 e 4 b 5 d

Vocabulary 4

1 documentary	4 TV series
2 sports programme	5 the news
3 comedy show	6 film

Vocabulary 5A

1 up	4 off
2 down	5 up
3 down	

Vocabulary 5B

1 turn up	4 turn off
2 stand up	5 turn down
3 sit down	

Extend your vocabulary

1 see	4 see
2 watch	5 see
3 watch	6 watch

Pronunciation 1

1 rich	6 his
2 leave	7 it
3 steal	8 he's
4 live	9 reach
5 eat	10 still

Pronunciation 2

1 Can you turn <u>up</u> the radio?
2 Please sit <u>down</u>.
3 Don't turn <u>off</u> the computer!
4 We stand <u>up</u> when the teacher comes in.
5 Turn <u>down</u> that TV!
6 Sit <u>down</u> and listen to me.
7 Turn <u>off</u> the television. It's time to go to bed.

Listening

1 False – she says 'I don't watch Hollywood films very often.'
2 True – she says 'I prefer independent films.'
3 True – she says 'You can see how other people around the world live and how they see the world.'
4 False – about world cinema she says 'I love listening to other languages too.'
5 False – he thinks some independent films are sad.
6 False – Mei says Hollywood films don't have any new ideas.
7 True – she says 'The Hollywood version's boring.'
8 True – he says 'And they have my favourite actors.' and this is a positive comment.

Reading

1
The student's own answer.

2
A soap opera is a TV drama series. Soap operas are popular in the US, the UK, Australia, South America, Spain, Europe, Asia, the Arab world.

3
1 radio
2 soap manufacturers
3 the US / the 1930s
4 the 1930s / the US
5 closed, open
6 telenovelas

4
1 False – the basic format is the same.
2 True
3 True
4 False – each episode continues a story from the last episode.
5 False – they are translated into other languages too.
6 True

5
1 They are the world's most popular type of TV programme.
2 The soap opera *Guiding Light* is the world's longest story.

6
1 e 2 c 3 a 4 b 5 d

7

1 four days a week	4 sometimes
2 always	5 often
3 once a year	

Writing

1
1 It's an old programme.
2 It's on every night.
3 It's in Alaska.
4 He wants to be a film director.
5 Because the characters are interesting, you learn a lot about people and life, and it's quite funny.

2
1 TV channel, time
2 place
3 people and situation
4 name of character

3

1 really	3 very
2 a little	4 quite

Answer Key

Unit 6

Grammar 1A
1 can't
2 can't
3 can
4 can
5 can
6 can't

Grammar 1B
1 Can she use
2 she can't
3 can walk
4 can she make
5 she can
6 can't phone
7 can we go
8 we can't

Grammar 2
1 Can you type
2 can
3 can type
4 Can you speak
5 can't
6 Can I ask
7 Can you give
8 can

Grammar 3A
1 good
2 well
3 easy
4 quickly
5 quickly
6 slow

Grammar 3B
1 perfectly
2 well
3 easily
4 badly
5 slowly
6 quickly

Grammar 4A
1 were
2 were
3 wasn't
4 was
5 were
6 weren't
7 were
8 was

Grammar 4B
1 wasn't
2 weren't
3 were
4 was
5 were
6 weren't
7 wasn't
8 was

Grammar 5A
1 were
2 were
3 was
4 Was
5 wasn't
6 were
7 Were
8 were
9 were

Grammar 5B
1 Was she
2 wasn't
3 was she
4 Were
5 were
6 were her ideas
7 was she
8 was her name

Vocabulary 1A
1 scientist
2 teacher
3 architect
4 doctor
5 lawyer
6 engineer

Vocabulary 1B
1 doctor
2 office worker
3 scientist
4 architect
5 engineer
6 sports coach
7 teacher
8 lawyer

Vocabulary 2
Across	Down
2 draw	1 play
3 swim	2 drive
4 dance	3 sing

Vocabulary 3A
1 law school
2 kindergarten
3 medical college
4 secondary school
5 technical college
6 college
7 boarding school
8 elementary school

Vocabulary 3B
1 university
2 high
3 primary
4 nursery
5 law
6 technical
7 library

Vocabulary 4A
1 geography
2 chemistry
3 PE
4 maths
5 history
6 ICT

Vocabulary 4B
1 biology
2 history
3 geography
4 languages
5 chemistry
6 physics

Extend your vocabulary
1 Peter was a bit lazy at school.
2 My home town is a little bit rough.
3 The film *The Sixth Sense* is a little bit scary.
4 I like maths but it's a bit difficult.
5 This mobile's great but it's a bit expensive.
6 It was a little bit boring.

Pronunciation 1
1 b /kɑːnt/
2 a /kən/
3 b /kɑːnt/
4 a /kən/
5 a /kən/
6 b /kæn/

Pronunciation 2
	First	Second
1 physics	✔	
2 language	✔	
3 teacher	✔	
4 pencil	✔	
5 English	✔	
6 hotel		✔
7 doctor	✔	
8 lawyer	✔	
9 thriller	✔	
10 cartoon		✔
11 August	✔	
12 July		✔

Listening
1 a parent or teacher
2 well
3 unfriendly
4 near their house
5 a lot of different countries
6 meet other children

Reading
1
The student's own answers.
2
1 Germany
2 teacher
3 Physics
4 violin
3
1 wasn't
2 wasn't
3 wasn't
4 was
5 can't
6 was
7 was
8 don't have
4
1 Later
2 First, Then
3 From
4 before, after
5
1 possibly
2 quickly
3 well
4 constantly
5 immediately

Writing
1
Teaching English as a foreign language.
2
1 Ray Chén Yam-kuen
2 Hong Kong
3 change his job and travel to other countries
4 an official qualification
5 He works in an office
6 He studied English at university
7 he speaks English very well.
8 an assistant teacher in an English school
3
1 so
2 because
3 because
4 so
5 so
4
1 on
2 for, in
3 in
4 at
5 at
6 of
7 for

Answer Key

Unit 7

Grammar 1A

1 started **5** carried
2 decided **6** published
3 used **7** created
4 produced

Grammar 1B

1 presented **4** watched
2 listened **5** studied
3 used **6** stopped

Grammar 2

1 d **2** f **3** b **4** e **5** a **6** c

Grammar 3A

Regular verbs	
Infinitive	**Past simple**
answer	*answered*
ask	asked
phone	phoned
stop	stopped
spy	spied
walk	walked

Irregular verbs	
Infinitive	**Past simple**
get	got
go	went
have	had
hear	heard
leave	left
make	made
see	saw
write	wrote

Grammar 3B

1 heard **5** saw
2 made **6** had
3 went **7** knew
4 got **8** became

Grammar 4

1 It's 6 am **5** I like it
2 It's sunny **6** No, it isn't
3 it's cold **7** Yes, it is
4 It's great **8** It has good views

Grammar 5A

1 Where did you go?
2 How did you travel?
3 Who did you go with?
4 Did you have a good time?
5 What did you do there?
6 Did you swim in the sea?

Grammar 5B

1 did you go **5** Did your son visit
2 Did you **6** didn't
3 Did you **7** did you like
4 did **8** did it feel

Grammar 6

1 didn't go **5** didn't know
2 didn't have **6** didn't stay
3 didn't visit **7** didn't write
4 didn't see **8** didn't get

Vocabulary 1

1 on **7** in
2 In **8** In
3 in **9** to
4 at **10** in
5 at **11** in
6 in **12** to

Extend your vocabulary

1 story **4** story
2 history **5** story
3 history

Vocabulary 2A

1 rain **4** sun
2 wind **5** freezing
3 clouds

Vocabulary 2B

1 cold **5** sunny
2 freezing **6** rainy
3 warm **7** snowy
4 boiling **8** windy

Pronunciation 1

	-ed is an extra syllable: /ɪd/	*-ed* isn't an extra syllable
1 I visited Hanoi.	✔	
2 I stayed at a hotel.		✔
3 I wanted to see an old friend.	✔	
4 I looked for his number.		✔
5 I picked up the phone.		✔
6 I phoned his number.		✔
7 I waited.	✔	
8 The answer phone started.	✔	
9 I listened to the message.		✔
10 The message ended.	✔	
11 I decided to leave a message.	✔	
12 He called me the next day.		✔

Pronunciation 2

1 2 **2** 3 **3** 4 **4** 4 **5** 3 **6** 3

Listening

1 Speaker 2 **6** Speaker 3
2 Speaker 1 **7** Speaker 1
3 Speaker 3 **8** Speaker 3
4 Speaker 1 **9** Speaker 2
5 Speaker 2

Reading

1
stratus, cumulonimbus, cirrus
2
1 They're made of drops of water and sometimes ice crystals.
2 It's an invisible gas.
3 Water vapour becomes liquid.
4 It collects on dust particles.
5 Fog.
6 He suggested Latin names for clouds.
3
1 cirrus
2 cumulus
3 stratus
4
1 didn't have **4** wasn't / was not
2 didn't understand **5** used
3 wrote **6** started

Writing

1
1 d **2** a **3** c **4** b
2
1 six days
2 every year, one year in France and the next year in Spain
3 extremely hot and sunny
4 a huge storm
5 in the dining room of a hotel
6 wasn't there, the wind blew it away during the night
3
1 the weather **4** rain
2 the temperature (hot) **5** wind
3 a storm
4
✔beautiful, ✔great, ✔wonderful
5
That night, At first, A little later, In the end, The next morning, during the night

Answer Key

Unit 8

Grammar 1A

1 doing
2 phoning
3 sitting
4 driving
5 swimming
6 waiting
7 working
8 using

Grammar 1B

1 are you going
2 'm / am going
3 're / are walking
4 's / is using
5 Are your children walking
6 's / is taking
7 aren't / are not working
8 isn't / is not raining
9 're / are going

Grammar 2

1 do you do
2 are you doing
3 I'm travelling
4 Does the 55 go
5 I'm reading
6 studies, 's studying

Grammar 3A

1 cheaper
2 happier
3 noisier
4 hotter
5 better
6 busier
7 more interesting
8 larger

Grammar 3B

1 warmer than Canada
2 nicer than work
3 sunnier than Scotland
4 bigger than buses
5 more expensive than bikes
6 worse than summer weather

Grammar 4A

1 c 2 a 3 e 4 b 5 f 6 d

Grammar 4B

1 to help
2 to see
3 to teach
4 to communicate
5 to have

Vocabulary 1A

1 train
2 on foot
3 metro
4 bicycle / bike
5 motorcycle / motorbike
6 boat

Vocabulary 1B

1 bike / bicycle
2 metro
3 foot
4 motorcycle / motorbike
5 boat
6 train

Vocabulary 2A

1 e 2 h 3 a 4 f 5 c 6 g 7 b 8 d

Vocabulary 2B

1 thousand
2 three thousand six hundred
3 sixty-eight thousand
4 four hundred and seventy-nine thousand
5 forty-eight thousand three hundred and eighty-one
6 two thousand seven hundred and fifty

Extend your vocabulary

1 come
2 coming
3 going
4 come
5 going
6 come
7 go
8 coming

Vocabulary 3A

1 happy
2 nervous
3 angry
4 bored
5 worried
6 sad

Vocabulary 3B

1 happy
2 sad
3 worried
4 nervous
5 bored
6 angry

Vocabulary 4

1 camera
2 credit card
3 passport
4 wallet
5 suitcase
6 toothbrush

Pronunciation 1

1 England's in the United Kingdom.
2 They're having a meeting in Singapore.
3 I think there's something in the fridge.
4 We're watching a boring film.
5 This evening we want to sing in a karaoke bar.
6 He's travelling to China by train.

Pronunciation 2

1 /həv/ (weak form)
2 /hæv/ (strong form)
3 /tuː/ (strong form)
4 /tə/ (weak form)
5 /kən/ (weak form)
6 /kæn/ (strong form)
7 /ðiː/ (strong form)
8 /ðə/ (weak form)

Listening

1 Do
2 Stand up
3 Sit
4 Drink
5 Don't drink
6 Change

Reading

1
1 c 2 b 3 d 4 a
2
The Quinghai-Tibet Railway
3
1 9:30 2 22:30 3 815 4 1,956
4
1 The weather in Xining is often cold and windy.
2 It's higher than all other railways in the world.
3 To not feel bad at Tanggula Pass, a lot of passengers need oxygen.
4 The second section of the track took 22 years to build.
5 The writer can't see the Himalayas when he arrives in Lhasa because it's dark.
6 He didn't use oxygen on the journey.
7 He has a positive opinion of the journey.
5
The transport network in China is growing. An example of this is the Qinghai-Tibet railway. This goes from Xining to Lhasa. The journey takes longer than a day to complete. A lot of tourists go to Lhasa to see the Potala palace, the traditional home of Tibet's Dalai Lamas.

Writing

1
2
1 Getting to the city
2 Travelling in the city
3 Places to stay
3
1 It takes 50 minutes.
2 They can travel by bus or hire a car.
3 It's best to travel by bus or on foot because the city centre's quite small and the buses are very efficient.
4 It's sometimes difficult to find a taxi in the evening.
4
1 bed-and-breakfast
2 youth hostel
3 hotel
4 guest house
5
1 to get
2 to park
3 to find
6
1 c 2 a 3 d 4 e 5 b

Answer Key

Unit 9

Grammar 1A
1 swum, swum
2 ridden, ridden
3 worked, worked
4 visited, visited
5 taken, taken
6 climbed, climbed

Grammar 1B
1 Have you planned
2 have
3 Have you ever seen
4 haven't
5 's / has travelled
6 Has he seen
7 hasn't
8 's / has visited
9 hasn't / has not visited
10 haven't decided

Grammar 2A
1 best   5 nicest
2 oldest   6 most traditional
3 most exciting   7 funniest
4 biggest   8 dirtiest

Grammar 2B
1 Correct
2 Incorrect – The correct form is the most important.
3 Correct
4 Incorrect – The correct form is more exciting because this is a comparative.
5 Incorrect – The correct form is are often the happiest.
6 Correct

Grammar 3A
1 I've got / I have got
2 They've got / They have got
3 Tom's got / Tom has got
4 He hasn't got / has not got
5 Have you got
6 Has your brother got

Grammar 3B
1 's got / has got
2 Has she got
3 hasn't / has not
4 's got / has got
5 Have they got
6 have
7 hasn't got / has not got
8 have not got / haven't got
9 Have you got
10 haven't

Grammar 4
1 one   6 ones
2 one   7 one
3 ones   8 one
4 ones   9 one
5 ones

Vocabulary 1A
1 lake   4 river
2 insect   5 bird
3 farm   6 plant

Vocabulary 1B
Across   **Down**
1 park   1 plant
3 mountain   2 zoo
5 bird   4 animal
7 farm   6 insect
9 lake   7 fish
10 tree   8 river

Vocabulary 2A
1 was   5 left
2 left   6 got
3 graduated   7 had
4 started   8 retired

Vocabulary 2B
1 born   5 had
2 left   6 left
3 work   7 graduated
4 married   8 from

Vocabulary 3A
1 arm   4 foot
2 hand   5 head
3 leg   6 shoulder

Vocabulary 3B
1 chest   5 back
2 arms   6 head
3 legs   7 feet
4 stomachs   8 shoulders

Vocabulary 4
1 mouth   5 nose
2 ears   6 hair
3 eyes   7 face
4 cheeks

Vocabulary 5A
1 skirt   4 gloves
2 jumper   5 trousers
3 scarf   6 shirt

Vocabulary 5B
1 socks   4 trousers
2 T-shirt   5 shorts
3 jeans   6 hat

Extend your vocabulary
1 light   4 light
2 dark   5 light
3 dark   6 dark

Pronunciation
1 socks   4 swim
2 skirt   5 sisters
3 see   6 stomach

Listening

	Trad	Eco	Trad & Eco
1	✔		
2		✔	
3		✔	
4			✔
5		✔	
6	✔		
7	✔		
8		✔	
9			✔
10	✔		

Reading
1
The student's own answers.
2
1 True.
2 False – it has been common around the world.
3 False – they were in the ears.
4 True.
5 False – men and women had piercings in the past.
3
1 Status symbol   3 Getting married
2 Coming of age   4 Fashion
4
1 To help have children (in India)
2 To make a face scarier (in some Pacific cultures)
3 To make a person more beautiful (in Malawi)
4 For religious reasons (in Mali)
5
1 've / have got   4 got married
2 the oldest   5 Have / been
3 ones   6 the best

Answer Key

Writing

1

b

2

1 False – he or she is from Europe.

2 True.

3 False – they have stayed with families.

4 True – it's at night because the speech starts with 'Good evening'.

5 False – he or she says there's still a lot of work to do.

3

1 I'd like to say a few words on behalf of …

2 First of all, I'd like to thank …

3 I'd also like to thank …

4 Thank you, too, for …

5 One final thing before I finish.

6 So, let's continue …

4

1 Thank you for organising this fantastic party.

2 I'd like to thank all my friends for coming this evening.

3 We'd like to say thank you for all your help.

4 Thank you Jack and Tina for travelling all the way from Canada.

Answer Key

Unit 10

Grammar 1A
1 Doing
2 help
3 exercise
4 running
5 get
6 choosing
7 Choose
8 doing

Grammar 1B
1 reading
2 talking
3 Doing
4 using
5 turning
6 Meeting
7 winning
8 playing

Grammar 2A
1 are going to visit
2 isn't / is not going to see
3 aren't / are not going to watch
4 are going to eat
5 's / is going to swim
6 isn't / is not going to go

Grammar 2B
1 are you going to do
2 'm / am going to watch
3 Is Tania going to see
4 is
5 Are you going (to go)
6 isn't / is not going to stay
7 Are you going to have
8 'm not / am not
9 'm / am going to have

Grammar 3A
1 was
2 won
3 has organised
4 was
5 has usually taken
6 has selected
7 has played
8 played

Grammar 3B
1 started
2 gave
3 's / has played
4 hasn't / has not won
5 was
6 hasn't / has not stopped
7 got
8 's / has decided

Vocabulary 1A

do	read	play
nothing	books	board games
puzzles	comics	cards
sport	newspapers	video games

Vocabulary 1B
1 books
2 newspapers
3 puzzles
4 sports
5 video games
6 comics

7 cards
8 board games
9 nothing

Extend your vocabulary 1
1 fun
2 funny
3 fun
4 funny
5 fun
6 funny

Vocabulary 2A
1 market
2 sports stadium
3 shop
4 castle
5 church
6 airport

Vocabulary 2B
1 monument
2 church
3 art gallery
4 castle
5 market
6 beach
7 museum
8 sports stadium
9 theatre

Vocabulary 3A
1 skiing
2 basketball
3 volleyball
4 running
5 cycling
6 football

Vocabulary 3B
1 play
2 play
3 go
4 play
5 go
6 play
7 go
8 go
9 play

Extend your vocabulary 2
1 careless
2 painful
3 helpful
4 careful
5 painless
6 beautiful

Vocabulary 4
1 objective
2 points
3 win
4 lose
5 cheating
6 turn

Pronunciation
1 she
2 take
3 phoned
4 you
5 hair
6 three
7 her
8 boat
9 sports
10 game

Listening
1 a 2 b 3 a 4 b 5 a 6 b

Reading
1
The student's own answers.
2
1 is 2 is 3 have 4 can
3
1 Because it shows the rest of the planet that a country has power.

2 It isn't clear (where it started).
3 It comes from *shah*, the Persian word for *king*.
4 They developed in southern Europe.
5 You need to decide your tactics.
6 The two things can make our brains younger.
7 Because it was the perfect way to test their computers.

4
1 Chess arrived in southern Europe.
2 The first modern chess tournament, in London.
3 Wilhelm Steinitz was the first official World Champion.
4 The computer *Deep Blue* played the world champion Garry Kasparov and won.

5
1 has become (paragraph 1), have been (paragraph 3), have seen (paragraph 4)
2 globe, planet (paragraph 1)
3 most popular (paragraph 1), the best (paragraph 5)
4 for making (paragraph 4)
5 you are going to do (paragraph 4)
6 won (paragraph 5)

6
1 were
2 have learned
3 Playing
4 are going to find
5 winning
6 are going to win

Writing
1
informal
2
1 Jess
2 New Delhi, India
3 Lou,
4 Sydney (Australia)
5 She's seen the Taj Mahal.
6 She's going to walk around the old city, visit the Red Fort and go to bed early.
7 She's going to visit two cities in Rajasthan.

3

At the start	At the end
Hi …	All the best,
Dear …	Take care,
	Love,
	Best wishes,

4
1 How's it going
2 What about you
3 by the way
4 Let me know
5 Anyway

5
1 plan to visit
2 're going to
3 're going to walk

Macmillan Education
Between Towns Road, Oxford OX4 3PP
A division of Macmillan Publishers Limited

Companies and representatives throughout the world

ISBN 978-0-230-42932-1

First published 2011

Designed by eMC Design Limited
Cover design by Macmillan Publishers Ltd
Cover photos (front and back) by permission of the Museum of the History
of Science, University of Oxford/Keiko Ikeuchi.

The authors and publishers would like to thank the following for permission
to reproduce their photographs:
Bananastock; Brand X; Comstock; Corbis; Creatas; Digital Stock; Digital
Vision; Getty; Goodshoot; Grapheast; Image 100; Image Source; iStock;
Macmillan Publishers Ltd; Medio Images; Pathfinder; Photoalto; Photodisc;
Stockbyte

These materials may contain links for third party websites. We have no
control over, and are not responsible for, the contents of such third party
websites. Please use care when accessing them.

Although we have tried to trace and contact copyright holders before
publication, in some cases this has not been possible. If contacted we will be
pleased to rectify any errors or omissions at the earliest opportunity.

Printed in Thailand

2015 2014 2013 2012
10 9 8 7 6 5 4 3 2